UNLOCK THE WEALTH MINDSET
Master Money Habits

Reena Saxena

UNLOCK YOUR WEALTH MINDSET – Master Money Habits

Self-published book

Cover Design by Deep Saxena, Partner – Mintage Events

ISBN: **978-93-340-0686-5**

Printed in India

For permissions, contact:

info@moneygoalz.com

First Edition: February, 2024

Dedicated to all those who shared personal stories about money and enriched my perspective. They helped my thought process branch into several directions, as I worked at finding patterns in apparently distinctive situations.

You will never know you helped me, but you have my gratitude forever.

PROLOGUE – UNLEASHING FINANCIAL POTENTIAL

Over the past 25 years, I have worked in the banking industry, helping countless individuals and families manage their finances and achieve their goals. Through my experience as a financial coach, trainer, and writer, I have witnessed first-hand the power of mindset in shaping our financial lives.

I saw all this happening at close quarters, across the table. The purpose of negotiating rates, expecting special treatment, flaunting or hiding wealth, small errors leading to major financial mishaps, and consistency leading to overall prosperity – every act was the result of a certain mindset. When money mindsets clash, relationships change. A shift in perspective can lead to a domino effect of positive changes, opening doors to possible opportunities.

Now, I want to share my knowledge and insights with you. I invite you to embark on this journey with me that will transform your financial life and deepen your understanding of wealth and abundance.

But before we dive into the practical strategies and techniques, I think setting the tone for this book is important. I want to create an environment where you feel supported, inspired, and empowered to take control of your financial destiny.

In our society, money is often seen as a taboo subject. We shy away from discussing it openly, citing privacy reasons, or hiding a fear of being seen as too materialistic. But I believe that by embracing money as an integral part of our lives and understanding its true nature, we can unlock its full potential and manifest abundance.

Money by itself is not vile. It places a lot of power in the owner's hands which is mis-utilized by some. And these few miscreants give money a bad reputation. How does an honest, enterprising individual succeed in life, but with the help of hard-earned and well-invested money?

Imagine a world where everyone has a healthy relationship with money - where we view it as a tool for creating opportunities, supporting our dreams, and positively impacting the world. Money is integrated into our lives and works with other elements to maximize returns. It is not a subject to deal with in isolation. And this is possible, only with the help of the right money habits – habits that hold your family, lifestyle, financial goals, and success together.

Throughout this book, I will guide you through a series of thought-provoking exercises, powerful techniques, and insightful stories from my life and the lives of others who have successfully transformed their relationship with money. I will also draw on the latest research in psychology, neuroscience, and personal development to comprehensively understand the wealth mindset. But this journey is not just about acquiring knowledge. It is about taking action and implementing what you learn. Each chapter includes actionable steps that you can immediately apply to your life, allowing you to make meaningful progress on your path to financial abundance.

As we move forward together, I encourage you to approach this journey with an open mind and a willingness to challenge your existing beliefs and patterns. Transformation rarely happens by staying within our comfort zones. It requires us to step out into the unknown, to confront our fears, and to embrace change.

I understand that change can be scary. It can feel overwhelming and uncertain. However small steps taken consistently over time can lead to significant change. If you need validation, there is always a financial coach, financial planner, habit coach, accountability partner, or author to support you.

Finally, I want to remind you that this journey is not just about money. It is about creating a life of purpose, contentment, and joy. Financial abundance is not an end in itself; it is a means to an end - a means to live the life you truly desire, to explore your passions, to contribute to your community, and to experience a deep sense of freedom and empowerment.

So, my dear reader, are you ready to embark on this transformative journey towards financial abundance? Are you ready to unlock your wealth mindset and manifest the life of your dreams? If your answer is yes, then I invite you to turn the page and begin this remarkable adventure with me. Together, we will uncover the hidden treasures within you and set sail toward a future filled with abundance, prosperity, and joy.

Welcome to the journey. Let's begin.

CHAPTER 1

FINANCIAL IQ BOOST – THE POWER OF HABIT

Habits are the actions you perform or decisions you take daily, as a part of your daily routine.

By and large, you can divide a major part of your acts during the day into three categories. This does not include thoughtful acts or decision-making. It is about what you mostly do on autopilot mode. And this is what constitutes your lifestyle.

1. MECHANICAL HABITS

You brush your teeth, bathe, drive to work, and have tea, coffee, and your meals without thinking.

2. DISCRETIONARY HABITS

You make a choice. You exercise and eat healthy to remain fit. You dress in a certain manner and drive a car to declare your social status.

3. IDENTITY HABITS

You perform certain actions because you identify yourself in a certain way.

1. *A shopkeeper bills me less due to a calculation error. When I realize it, I drive back a few miles to pay the balance. It is because I am honest.*

I identify myself as an honest person. I will not be true to myself if I do something else.

2. *I dress formally because that is how people working in the finance domain are expected to dress.*

I identify myself as a finance professional.

But I dress relaxed while attending literary events or writers' group meetings. My persona has changed.

CAN WE CHANGE OUR HABITS?

Yes. We need to do something different, till the action gets embedded in our daily routines.

Coaches talk about 21- 45 days to create a new habit. It may take longer than that, depending on how much time it takes to get embedded in your subconscious.

Why should I do it?

What is the driving force to make me change?

I may start and discontinue after some time, as it happens with New Year Resolutions, gym routines, or healthy eating habits.

Change needs to be incentivized with a clearly defined goal. The drive to achieve that goal should override all other reasons to break the resolution.

How should I do it?

- ☐ Identify the trigger points which make you act in a certain way. Change the triggers.
- ☐ You indulge in alcohol, cigars, or junk food **when your friends come over.**
- ☐ Would you still do it, in the absence of friends?
- ☐ Understanding the mechanism correctly will help you devise an action plan to overcome it.

What happens when I change?

Does change have an impact on my identity?

Change the identity.

- **What will people say if they see me cycling to work?**

Do you like to be known as a fitness-conscious person, or a prosperous person who owns a fancy car?

- **What will someone think if they see me dressed casually?**

Let them think I'm a creative writer, an artist, and a freelancer other than working in the finance domain. Let them see me as a relaxed boss who does not waste time on clothes.

- **There is a difference between the following two sentences.**

I'm trying to give up alcohol.

I am a teetotaller.

In the latter case, a paradigm shift has happened. The identity has changed. Now, it has become easier to adopt the new habit.

Let's see how this extends to money habits in the next piece.

KEY TAKEAWAYS

1. **Habits Overview**

Habits encompass daily actions and decisions forming a routine. The three main categories are Mechanical, Discretionary, and Identity.

2. **Changing Habits**

Change is possible by introducing new actions into daily routines. Coaches suggest 21-45 days for habit formation. Incentives and clearly defined goals are crucial for sustaining change.

3. **Driving Change**

Identifying trigger points for actions and modifying them. Understanding mechanisms behind habits to devise effective action plans.

4. **Impact of Change**

The change affects personal identity. Shifting from trying to adopt a new habit involves a paradigm shift.

CHAPTER 2

DECODING SECRETS TO WEALTH – WHAT ARE MONEY HABITS?

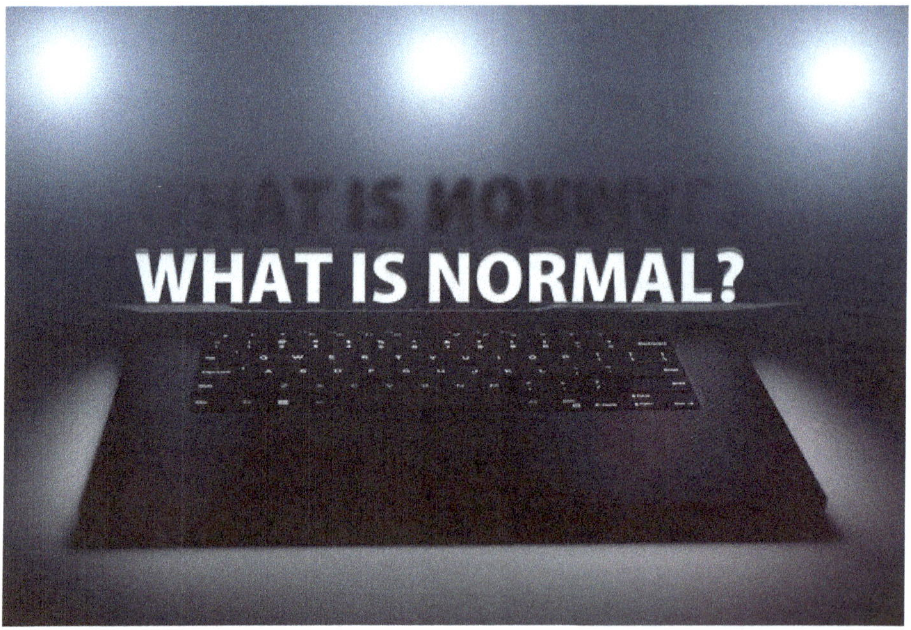

Money habits are often confused with spending habits.

Spending is an act that creates money patterns in our lives. It is not the pattern.

We save money by deciding not to spend.

We spend money by deciding not to save.

How does one decision override another?

SUBCONSCIOUS IMPRINTS

Amy Carlson, a Coach from Norway narrates this incident from her childhood. When she asked for expensive white boots, her mother told her she was not worth it.

The idea got ingrained in her subconscious. She finds herself spending on her home, family, and dogs but not on herself.

She says behavior patterns about money get ingrained before the age of seven years.

Soma buys only the best because her mother always derided those using cheap stuff – "Yuck, how can they?" At that moment, affordability does not matter. Living by a certain mental model does matter.

People buy larger houses than they can afford, and let the EMIs drain their finances because they have set up a 'minimum' benchmark for lifestyles. The idea of dropping below that point is anathema.

Whatever our parents say in childhood, becomes our inner voice, but we are unaware of it.

WHY IS IT DIFFICULT TO CHANGE THOUGHT PATTERNS?

We do not go with the merit of an idea, facts, or thoughts. We go with our sense of belonging to a certain tribe. It can be your community, family, social circle, or anyone you admire and follow. Doing something that contradicts itself feels disloyal.

You want to belong. You don't want to get thrown out of the tribe. So much of what we do in life is to maintain affiliation, follow rules, and not stand out like a sore thumb.

We wait for others to change, a few people to nudge us and then we may do something to change behavior patterns.

We go with the identity we have established for ourselves.

A former MNC CXO, once mentioned how she identified herself with her pay packet, and it dictated behavior patterns after she quit the job. She would be sitting in a café with a former colleague, and thinking, "Do I have the right to sip this exorbitant amount for a coffee? She is earning, and I'm not." She could well afford the coffee, but a pang of guilt about not being financially independent was gnawing at her.

She took time to rediscover and redefine herself when she became a business coach and could help others make money.

IS IT POSSIBLE TO CHANGE?

We need to become aware of the thought patterns that drive our actions first.

You will move in the following order to change your mindset.

- ☐ Awareness
- ☐ Acceptance
- ☐ Identify triggers
- ☐ Reset response
- ☐ Develop a system
- ☐ Work in communities

We'll discuss this in future interactions.

KEY TAKEAWAYS

1. **Decision-Making Dynamics**

The author delves into the dynamics of decision-making regarding money, highlighting the paradox of saving by choosing not to spend and spending by choosing not to save.

2. **Subconscious Imprints**

The narrative includes an anecdote about how childhood experiences, particularly parental influence, can leave lasting imprints on one's subconscious, impacting spending behavior later in life.

3. **Influence of Early Experiences**

The chapter suggests that behavior patterns related to money are often ingrained before the age of seven, with examples illustrating how parental comments during childhood can become internalized and influence financial decisions.

4. **Challenges in Changing Thought Patterns**

The difficulty in changing thought patterns is explored, attributing resistance to a sense of belonging and loyalty to certain tribes, such as family or social circles. The process involves changing mindset, involving awareness, acceptance, trigger identification, response reset, system development, and community engagement.

CHAPTER 3

DISCOVER YOUR WEALTH CODE – IDENTIFYING MONEY HABITS

What do they reveal about you?

Money habits are what you normally do in a given set of circumstances, unconsciously, in autopilot mode. Let us check out some money habits examples.

WHAT MONEY HABITS DO YOU HAVE?

Check your bank statements for the last six months. See what they say about your money habits.

1. On which date did you pay your bills? Was it before the due date, on the due date, or after the due date with a late fee?
2. How many times do you order groceries? What is the average size of the bill?
3. What is the frequency of ordering food online? How much do you spend on an average per order?
4. Do you like shopping online or offline? What have you purchased and how many times?
5. Would you prefer to pay in cash, by card, net banking, or a payment app?
6. How often do you withdraw cash from an ATM?
7. Have you given money to charity or lent it to someone else?
8. Are some of the expenses influenced by people you know? Did a friend ask you to buy something she is promoting or selling? Maybe you splurged on food and flowers, just before the arrival of a guest. Or you bought an expensive outfit to attend a special event you feel lucky to have been invited to?

9. Does your family influence you into spending more than you can afford? How do you compensate for shortfalls elsewhere?

10. What is your first response when someone else offers to pay or brings a gift?

- *That's great!*
- *Of course, I can't accept something so expensive.*
- *Thank you! I'll wait for my turn to return the favor.*

Honest answers to the above will tell you a lot about yourself.

WHAT DO THESE HABITS REVEAL ABOUT YOU?

1. PAYING BILLS ON TIME

Some people see it as a non-negotiable duty. Others pay to avoid penalties. There are yet others who think they can use the money elsewhere for some gain. Bills can wait for some time.

These things are coming into regulatory focus now. The Public Credit Registry managed by the Reserve Bank of India records whether bills and taxes are paid on time, and if there are any cheque return cases filed against the individual. It is a 360-degree assessment of the individual. A defaulter tends to exhibit the same behavior on multiple platforms.

2. ORDERING GROCERIES

You feel insecure if the larder is poorly stocked. You are fastidious about laying an interesting table for your family or guests.

Rita prefers buying stuff when needed and not overstocking the fridge. What are quick delivery services meant for? There is no wastage if she does not need it.

Heena does not feel good about ordering for less than Rs.1000/-. So, she adds up things not needed immediately, just to inflate the bill.

3. ORDERING FOOD OR ONLINE SHOPPING

Amita lives in the moment and wants immediate gratification. Good food and clothes or shoes boost a sense of well-being.

Roma thinks it's a waste of money, and she may not like what is delivered. Buying something is an investment and takes more thought and planning.

Online wandering, choosing and buying is a pastime for Nidhi.

4. MODE OF PAYMENT

Cash is cumbersome, but you stop to think and count before you part with it.

Althea is trigger-happy and uses only payment apps. Who will remember card numbers or take the trouble to log in to net banking?

Before making a payment, Tom changes the internet connection to a private one. He is safety conscious and does not want to fall prey to fraudulent use of online data.

5. BEING INFLUENCED BY OTHERS

What is the dominant thought when you give in to subtle hints or mounting pressure?

- ☐ Seeing it as a display of status
- ☐ Not wanting to disappoint the person you're emotionally attached to.
- ☐ Fear of conflict and turmoil. You prefer to buy peace.
- ☐ You think they will not understand your situation even if you explain
- ☐ A desire to keep your problems secret.

6. TAKING MONEY

Some people feel their self-respect is jeopardized by accepting money or help from others. It goes beyond independence. They don't want to be obliged, even if it is a rightful transaction. The self is very strongly defined, and it bounces off any suggestion or offer by others.

We've all met the types who negotiate their way through every deal – big or small. They want value for money.

There are yet others always on the lookout to grab something for free. Instant gratification matters more than self-worth or how others view them. If they want it, they will take it – by hook or crook.

KEY TAKEAWAYS

1. **Money Habits Assessment**

Examine your bank statements to understand your money habits. Consider bill payment timing, grocery and food orders, shopping preferences, and payment methods.

2. **Insights from Habits**

Routine activities like paying bills, ordering groceries, mode of payment, safety measures, and decision-making are indicators of your money value.

3. **Self-Reflection**

Honest answers to these habits reveal significant aspects of one's financial behavior and mindset. Understanding these habits provides insights into financial decision-making and priorities.

CHAPTER 4

WEALTH BLUEPRINT: UNVEILING SECRETS BEHIND RICHES

Old Money has legacy brands, they have their traditions, their favorite hotels, resorts, and automobile brands, and stick with

them.

New money is bold and wild and wants attention.

I asked this question in a workshop,

"What makes you feel rich?"

The answers varied from owning luxury yachts to vacation homes to just being debt-free.

Hence, I choose not to use the word 'Millionaire' which pops up in the titles of many wealth management books. A million dollars in Indian rupees is an amount that tags you as comfortable, but not exactly wealthy. So, let's set our targets for numbers, forgetting we counted among the wealthy.

HOW TO GET RICH AND STAY RICH?

What about feeling rich?

We often yearn for designer outfits or fancy cars owned by celebrities. Some of the outfits we see on TV shows are lent by designers to promote their brands. Owning it might make us feel rich, but let's think about the percentage of their annual income spent on that one outfit, and compare it with ours.

Getting into debt to own a fancy car or house or designer togs will not make us feel rich for long. Rich people do not receive frequent calls from debt recovery agents.

If you think building a house on a plot you own works out cheaper than buying a home in a posh locality, go for it. The rich prefer buying houses to building those, but largely because they utilize the time better in making more money than building houses. Is that the case with you?

We are not in the same boat. Imitation is not the right approach. Adaptation works.

Here, you gain clarity on 'being rich' and 'feeling rich'.

The money habits mentioned in all financial education books can be summed up into 5 points.

1. DO NOT SPEND BEFORE YOU EARN

Credit cards and Buy Now Pay Later schemes are good to get you reward points, if you pay the bills on the due date.

2. GET VALUE FOR MONEY

"Rich people negotiate their way through every deal". Peyush Bansal, Founder of Lenskart and angel investor expressed this on Shark Tank India.

A recent news clip showed Mukesh Ambani enquiring about the price of clothes they were buying for their grandchildren at Macy's New York. Ambani can afford to buy the whole of Macy's, but it is ingrained in him to check if they are getting value for money.

They buy expensive things to deliver value in the long run. A single pair of boots that lasts long is better than the cheap ones you need to replace every quarter.

Mukesh Ambani has no qualms about eating from roadside stalls because he doesn't need to prove anything to anyone. Sudha Murthy, wife of Infosys founder, a celebrated author, and mother-in-law of the Prime Minister of the UK claims she has not shopped for clothes in a long time.

It is the middle class that strives to be seen as well-off and ends up spending on worthless items in the process.

3. PAY YOUR FUTURE SELF FIRST

It just means whatever you wish to save for the future should be set aside first. Manage your expenses in the remaining amount.

Pay the insurance premiums, SIP installments, recurring deposits, contributions to the Public Provident Fund, and/or other small savings schemes first. Make a budget for routine expenses with the remaining amount.

4. DIFFERENTIATE BETWEEN NEEDS AND WANTS

We were talking about 'cost of living' and 'lifestyle costs' during the stay-at-home Corona phase. Have a budget for your wants. These are good to have discretionary items.

Are you aware that celebrities do not buy all the designer outfits and accessories they flaunt in public functions? Designers lend these expensive clothes for an evening to showcase their work. The celebrities effectively become clotheshorses for them.

Sustainable fashion is trending now and stars repeat or recycle outfits to drive a point.

5. CREATE ASSETS, NOT LIABILITIES

Anything that generates income or can be liquidated to get cash is an asset. It can be real estate for some, to yield income or a business. The house you live in should ideally not be counted. Time-saving gadgets which leave you free to earn more money can also be counted.

Anything that adds to your expenses is a liability. It can be a high-maintenance house or car.

How you incorporate these concepts into your money habits is subjective, and financial coaching can help.

6. CELEBRITIES ENCASH STAR VALUE

They know how business works. The organizer will sell highly-priced tickets if a popular figure is a part of the show just like the manufacturer will sell 30 pieces of a garment if an actor is seen flaunting it on social media.

So they charge for making an appearance.

They demand that the producer or organizer take care of their expenses during a foreign trip or shoot in outdoor locations.

KEY TAKEAWAYS

1. **Richness Perception**

Distinguish between being rich and feeling rich. Adapt to personal circumstances rather than imitating others.

2. **Wealth-Building Habits**

Earn before spending; manage credit wisely. Prioritize savings for the future over routine expenses. Differentiate between needs and wants. Create assets that generate income

3. **Individualized Financial Approach**

Applying financial concepts to personal habits is subjective. Seek financial coaching to align habits with long-term goals.

CHAPTER 5

WEALTH BLOCKERS – BREAKING FREE FROM HABITS THAT HINDER PROSPERITY

A friend shared an incident about giving an extra gas stove and a laundry iron to the maid. The maid's son sold both items for Rs.100/- and had ice cream with the money.

1. The man who bought it started ironing clothes on a table in a residential area to earn money. His wife used the extra gas stove to make snacks and sell them at the local store.

2. Financial literacy levels and spending habits of millennials can be shocking. When I ask students what they will do with a bonus of Rs. 1 lakh, most of them want to buy a MacBook and an iPhone and complain that the amount will not suffice. Only one guy presented a business plan of selling tea and snacks on a handcart, and then buying the coveted laptop and phone with the profits, after six months.

3. There are many such examples of money consumption habits. They just highlight a fundamental reason.

What keeps one rich poor or middle class is a short-term or long-term perspective.

AVOID THESE HABIT TRAPS LIKE THE C-VIRUS

• SEEKING IMMEDIATE GRATIFICATION

A seed cannot grow into a tree if it is consumed. Money does not become wealth unless it is saved and invested.

There are subconscious reasons for seeking immediate gratification. It can be suppressed desires, a difficult childhood,

FOMO (fear of missing out), or peer pressure.

Reckless use of credit cards and Buy Now Pay Later schemes, personal loans for vacation are all offshoots of this mindset. People spend their future income. Money grows, but in the lenders' bank accounts who earn hefty fees and interest on the deals.

The first step is to recognize and acknowledge the cause. One can work on solutions later.

• SOURCES OF INCOME

The commonest question on Quora or other social media platforms, is how to earn money before inculcating money habits, about getting that extra income to save and invest. What does one do in a hand-to-mouth situation, when the entire income is spent on fixed costs?

The concern is genuine and calls for ingenuity in finding resources and opportunities.

A business head ridicules team members who do not earn incentives. The derisive remark in review meetings "How can you survive on that measly salary?" makes people see red. Some go on the defensive and say they are not greedy.

I took some time to figure out that those who worked for incentives had a growth mindset. They had learned how to make an extra buck to invest, which would yield returns in the long run.

There is an old Marathi saying that the woman of the house should earn a minimal amount, equivalent to salt in food. Financially independent women earn a lot more than the proverbial pinch of salt, but the logic is about financial contributions from every capable member of the family. I see exceptional dignity of labor in certain communities. The stay-at-home members find some work to assist a businessperson or organization that can be done at home. Others take pride in flaunting their contribution.

Radha boasts about how they never gave pocket money to their chartered accountant son. He had learned to manage his expenses on the small stipend that he earned during article-ship. Summer jobs and paid internships are a lot more common now. Children become financially literate in the process and pay for the small comforts or luxuries they crave. They may also learn to invest.

Radha's son gave them a decent sum every month for household expenses, and she accepted it. A couple of years later, the son decided to buy an apartment in an upmarket residential colony. He shared his financial plan of availing a home loan and the margin money that he would pay. He was earning well and could easily afford the amount. But at this point, Radha intervened with a cheque for the down payment (margin money). It was all his money – the money that he gave his parents every month. She saved it all, as they were financially comfortable with her husband's pension. In true Indian style, he touched her feet and said, "Ma, you are Goddess Laxmi". (Laxmi is the Goddess of Wealth). He was learning his lessons in financial planning.

Expenses need not increase in direct proportion to income growth. Saving and investing for a long-term goal makes sense.

Actors and cricketers who invest money in other businesses know their success and career is short-lived. Needless to say, they emerge strong even after a professional lull. Their money works for them. They don't have to work for money all the time.

Having multiple sources of income is not only about part-time jobs or side hustles. Rent, interest, and dividends all count as sources of income but need capital. The money for capital needs to be earned and saved.

• VALUE SYSTEM

Some of us have grown up with the mindset that an overflowing refrigerator and overflowing wardrobes indicate prosperity. The thought of clearing up gives us goosebumps, because less is scary, and less is poverty.

We tend to miss the point that those who buy just enough for needs, and sell what is not needed have overflowing bank accounts. We need to make space in the cupboards for prosperity to find its way in, not overload them.

We need to make space for new goals and sources of income to enter.

• DEBT IS A MONEY-DRAINING HABIT

There is a social system that works at making you spend to maintain standards set by others. Weddings and ceremonies are just one example.

There is a financial system that lures you into borrowing by seemingly attractive deals (Pay only a minimum amount now...). They devise schemes with free credit for a limited period, to inculcate the debt habit. Buy Now Pay Later (BNPL) schemes are available for small expenses like ordering food on Zomato to buying high-priced consumer durables on Amazon.

I receive a minimum of three calls every day to offer me an overdraft or credit card that I don't need. The target prospect list is based only on the credit score, not the person's income, repaying capacity, or need.

People do give in to temptation, especially with loans being available online. A study conducted by the Reserve Bank of India shows that unsecured loans are recklessly distributed. A single borrower may have availed of 3-4 such loans. It does not speak well for his future credit scores or financial wellness, since the rates of interest are high. The money that should go towards investments is being squandered off in paying interest. Default in loan payments creates a scarier scenario.

The pride in the acquisition of a luxury asset or a memorable holiday far outweighs the astronomical interest outgo, but it makes you poorer in the long run, but the darker image has escaped your radar.

- **SUPERSTITION**

I'm horrified to see the amount poor people spend on godmen and exorcists, to solve every problem in their lives. It gets them nowhere, but the faith remains intact. They buy hope and miss out on long-term financial well-being.

Consequently, they always depend on wages and loans.

- **SOCIAL IMAGE**

50 Cent, an American rapper went broke in 2016, when he had to pay 23 million dollars to his creditors. His stance was that celebrities need to maintain a public image. His net worth in 2022 shows as $30 million, so he probably learned his lessons after that. His story might be a good lesson in narcissist spending habits and money management.

KEY TAKEAWAYS

1. **Avoid Immediate Gratification**

Consuming money instantly hinders wealth growth. Recognize and address underlying causes like FOMO or peer pressure. Credit card misuse and Buy Now Pay Later schemes impact future finances.

2. **Diversify Income Sources**

Seek ingenuity in resource-finding, especially in hand-to-mouth situations. Incentives and part-time work showcase a growth mindset. Financial literacy is key for exploring various income streams.

3. **Rethink Value Systems**

Overflowing possessions don't guarantee prosperity. Make room for new goals and income sources by decluttering. Challenge the mindset of associating abundance with material abundance.

4. **Beware of Debt Traps**

Social and financial systems promote spending beyond means. Attractive schemes, like Buy Now Pay Later, may lead to debt. Unsecured loans, especially online, can harm long-term financial health.

5. **Avoid Superstition and Image-driven Spending**

Spending on superstitions hampers long-term financial well-being. Dependence on wages and loans persists without rational financial planning. Celebrities' image maintenance can lead to financial pitfalls; prudent money management is crucial.

CHAPTER 6

HABIT MASTERY – NAVIGATING THE LOOP FOR FINANCIAL SUCCESS

Loops make life easier to understand, starting from childhood.

A baby masters the loop of

Feeling → Attracting Attention (with different sounds) → Expression → Gratification → Repetition

The process continues throughout our life, as we stick to rewarding behavior. Only disappointment drives us to break a loop. It is the pain of a certain action not being recognized or rewarded that takes us to the opposite end.

We rarely go off on a tangent into unexplored territory. When we do, we emerge as thinkers, artists, scientists, or writers.

Let's stick to daily life activities for now.

What are the three components of a habit loop?

Our life and behavior are dominated by three components

Emotion-Thought–Action

Let's take a few examples of habit loops.

Example 1

Emotion

I want to ace parenting

Thought

I'll do everything to keep my child happy

Action

I give in to unjustifiable demands not good for the child in the long run.

Example 2

Emotion

Fear of rejection, social isolation

Thought

I'm not acceptable without my outfit, car, gifts, or whatever I value

Action

I overspend on things I don't need

It need not always be negative.

Habit coaches talk about 'book-ending' behavior loops. If I dress in my gym clothes, I go to the gym and exercise. It ends with the desired outcome – the glow that exercise brings.

If I lounge around in night clothes for longer, the momentum is lost.

So, they advise focussing on the first step to get the rest of the process right.

HOW TO MAP HABIT LOOPS?

At times, breaking a negative habit automatically puts us in a positive mode.

I hear you sighing, "Only if that was so easy..."

Asking the right questions makes it easy, as we get to the root of the matter.

I want to buy this expensive robot for my child.

Why?

I want to see my child happy.

Why only with this robot?

I'm not able to spend enough time with my child.

How will this help?

My child remains busy.

Is there another way of ensuring that?

My child likes flaunting it to his friends.

Is that the value system you want to inculcate?

This is the easiest option for me as of now.

Does it make something else difficult for you?

Yes, my monthly spending budget goes for a toss.

Can it harm your child's long-term future?

Maybe. I'm saving and investing for her higher education.

What is the alternative?

Now, the solutions have started emerging. It may be about a new habit loop for your child or yourself. You know that guilt and busyness are driving you to this place.

Design similar questions for the second example.

What we are doing here is creating a new thinking habit, which decodes the underlying emotion. Action will follow.

ADAPTABILITY IS THE KEY

No habit is worth it if it harms your current or future interest. Maybe, it served you well in the past, but it is time to say Thank You and move on.

It takes time and effort to inculcate a new money habit.

At the same time, we need to be mentally prepared to abandon it for our benefit.

Goals are the driving force, and goalposts can move. We adapt to this in our professional life, as we give in to changing scenarios.

We don't want to do it in our personal life, because we want a comfort zone.

Ask the right question again.

Who says the next zone will not be comfortable?

We are not our minds. We find the picture or model of a brain baffling. The neurologist or doctor tells us all that your brain does.

So, it is an object which you can manoeuver just like the steering wheel of your car, to take you to the desired destination.

You are a fluid process, not a fixed thing.

> *A person is a fluid process, not a fixed and static entity; a flowing river of change, not a block of solid material; a continually changing constellation of potentialities, not a fixed quantity of traits.*
> ***— Carl Rogers, On Becoming a Person***

How long does it take for a new habit to kick in?

As long as it takes for your subconscious to accept the process, and put it in autopilot mode.

Once you acknowledge the power of your 'self' as different from the mind or other external/internal influencers, you are free.

KEY TAKEAWAYS

1. **Habit Loop Components**

Habit loops are formed through a continuous cycle of emotion, thought, and action.

2. **Book-Ending Behavior Loops**

Habit coaches recommend focusing on the first step to get the rest of the process right, emphasizing the impact of the initial action on the overall outcome.

3. **Mapping Habit Loops**

Breaking a negative habit can lead to a positive shift by asking the right questions and understanding the root causes.

4. **Self-awareness and Autopilot Mode**

Acknowledging the power of the self as distinct from the mind or external/internal influences is highlighted.

The goal is to reach a point where new habits are accepted by the subconscious and operate in autopilot mode.

5. **Timeline for Habit Formation**

The duration for a new habit to become ingrained is determined by the time it takes for the subconscious to accept the process and put it into autopilot mode.

CHAPTER 7

MOMENTS OF REVELATION – WHEN FINANCIAL CLARITY STRIKES

Whatever we call personality is a sum of our habits. It is how people see us, and form impressions about us.

And we are fine with it.

"Why should I want to change, if my life is smooth, and I don't cause harm to anyone else?"

Smoking and drinking are great fun habits, till they attack our wellness at a physical, financial, or relationship level.

The time we spend watching television or scrolling social media feeds mindlessly is entertaining, till other parts of our life suffer.

Spending or saving money gives a high. Why should it be a problem, if I use my own money and banks are competing to give me a loan?

What is that turning point in life when one feels a need to change? And meaningful change does not happen unless one reaches this point.

There are two types of habits: ones that comfort us, and ones that would be a comfort if we stopped.

Catherine Pulsifer

A successful actor once admitted to becoming more careful with money, when his father told him they won't have enough to pay medical bills in case of a serious illness. His estimates of his wealth were drastically incorrect.

I read posts from women in social media groups. They start counting money when the marriage fails and they are on the verge of separation. Money is taken for granted before that.

We are all conditioned to think about money in a certain way, as per T. Harv Eker

1. Verbal

By listening to statements made about money

2. Modelling

We behave in the same way, or exactly the opposite manner as we have seen our parents behave. The stance we take depends on our equation with them.

3. Blueprint

A blueprint can be identified and changed.

The oft-repeated example he gives is that of a lady, (let's call her Martha) whose daughter asked for money and her response was "Ask Dad."

This is the reply Martha always received from her mother in childhood. Despite being a career woman, she gave the same stock response to her daughter's request for money. The blueprint here was that men manage money matters.

WHEN DOES ONE WANT TO CHANGE SPENDING HABITS?

Let's look at some common occurrences when people feel a need to create healthy money habits.

- ☐ At a point close to retirement
- ☐ When you want to set an example for others
- ☐ During employment gaps
- ☐ On becoming a victim of fraud or cheating.
- ☐ After suffering a loss or downturn in business
- ☐ When Black Swan events alter your net worth
- ☐ You are strongly influenced by a mentor
- ☐ You've been denied a raise or a share in inheritance,

- ☐ Perspectives change towards the fag end of life
- ☐ Spirituality or asceticism makes you believe you can survive on much less

In short, a belief system is changing. Your assumptions and dreams are changing.

Your money blueprint is changing.

You know doing the same things will not yield different results.

Congratulations if you have reached this point!

Habits are never-ending goals, if you think about it. They have no deadline and no endpoint. They are casual daily activities like brushing your teeth or combing your hair.

Zoe McKey, Rewire Your Habits

I have witnessed firsthand how our beliefs about money and wealth can either propel us forward or hold us back. Our mindset plays a crucial role in our financial success. It is essential to identify and change any limiting beliefs we may have about money and wealth.

Limiting beliefs are deeply ingrained thoughts and assumptions that shape our perception of the world and ourselves. When it comes to money and wealth, these beliefs can be particularly influential. They often stem from societal conditioning, upbringing, and personal experiences, and can manifest in various ways.

One of the most common limiting beliefs about money is the belief that "money is the root of all evil." This belief is ingrained in our minds that money is a source of wrongdoing and immorality, which can create a subconscious aversion towards wealth. Another limiting belief is the notion that "rich people are greedy." This belief stereotypes wealthy individuals as selfish and unscrupulous, hindering our ability to aspire to financial abundance.

We discussed earlier that the power bestowed by money corrupts minds, not money itself.

These limiting beliefs have a profound impact on our mindset and our ability to manifest financial success. If we believe that money is inherently evil or that rich people are inherently greedy, we are likely to repel wealth instead of attracting it. Our actions, decisions, and choices are influenced by our beliefs, so it is crucial to challenge and reframe these limiting beliefs to align ourselves with abundance.

KEY TAKEAWAYS

1. **Habits Shape Personality:** Our habits, particularly those related to money, define our personality and may resist change until a significant event occurs.
2. **Impact of upbringing:** Beliefs about money are heavily influenced by upbringing and societal conditioning, often leading to the replication of parental behaviors.
3. **Turning Points Prompt Change:** Life events like nearing retirement, financial losses, or fraud can trigger a realization and the need to change spending habits.
4. **Money Blueprint:** Our beliefs about money are not fixed; they form a "money blueprint" that can be identified and changed.

5. **Challenge Limiting Beliefs:** Limiting beliefs about money, such as associating it with evil or viewing the wealthy as inherently greedy, need to be challenged and reframed for financial success.

CHAPTER 8

TRANSFORMATIVE CHANGE – MAKING HABITS WORK

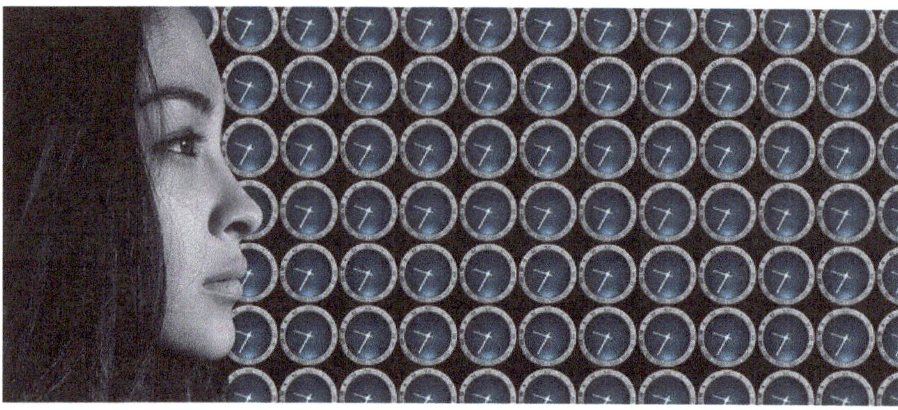

In the previous article, we discussed triggers that call for a change in money habits. It means that as long as there is no problem, one does not think about changing money habits or any habit.

A popular expression goes,

> ***Don't fix it, if it ain't broken.***

It is either a problem or a strong desire to be in a better place that catalyzes change.

But some people ask if it is possible to control spending habits. We've said before that money habits are set by age 7.

The truth is that there is no one-size-fits-all solution applicable to all. The only common factor is the realization that one needs to change. If a problem rises from the subconscious to the conscious mind, it is possible to work on it. If it remains submerged, behavior patterns are likely to remain the same.

Childhood Influence

Each child is born into a different set of challenges. We don't have to assume that only a lack of resources is a challenge. The problem of plenty is also a challenge, as the kids have not learned to work in a scenario of limited resources. The spending habits of millennials testify to this, as they are born in an era when money flows through devices, rather than savings accounts or piggy banks. Easy access creates a different set of habits than what their parents did.

I came across an intriguing statement from an heiress to a fortune. She said she feels inferior around people who have earned their fortunes, because she wouldn't know how to do it. So, she gives away money in charity to assuage guilt. But this behavior pattern by itself may be destructive. A Hindi saying goes that even 'Kuber ka Khazana' will be emptied if one does not add to it.

The financial sentiment formed at an early age becomes the basis of money habits. Most of the adults we meet have not been educated in money management by their parents or teachers.

Adulthood

Many people have made mistakes in the early stages, which may take a long time to overcome. Research shows that people who are in a financial mess, share many behavioral traits. The listicles on how to stop bad spending habits are often a summation of these.

We learn from collective experience but one may not need all of those measures. Or one may need something different from common solutions. There is no point confining ourselves in a templated system when it is possible to enjoy a higher degree of freedom.

MONEY MANAGEMENT SYSTEM

What is needed for change is a customized money management system.

Needless to say, a system based on hard-core financial information and Excel sheets alone will not suffice.

A financial coach needs to address established behavior and habits.

An actor in a low phase was unable to pay his loan installments. His wife pointed fingers at those who owed him money but were not paying up. She was sarcastic about her husband being called a perfect gentleman and nice person by the film industry.

His staff appeared grateful that they were retained and paid salaries regularly despite not having much work to do.

At the same time, he was being exploited by a so-called friend who lent money in need, but at an astronomical rate of interest.

The situation reflected a clash between different value systems. Finally, we found a solution by getting a customer to buy his upmarket apartment. He repaid the bank loan and moved to a lesser-priced house on the same street.

A strictly financial approach would lambast him for bloated manpower expenses. But his conscience did not permit him to sack people who stood by him through thick and thin.

Can people go against their DNA in making hard decisions?

Employees need to do it, but they quit at the earliest opportunity. Startup owners may be compelled by their investors to adopt unethical practices. Those arrangements last where the founder's mindset is transformed by the profit motive. If not, they need to look at alternative solutions or shut the shop.

The system needs to be customized to suit the individual for sustainability. The mental soil needs to be fertile and open to new seeds. The climate needs to be appropriate. Only then will trees grow and bear delicious fruits.

For example, a financial coaching conversation can start as follows.

1. What is it about spending money that makes you feel good?
2. What will happen if you do not indulge in this behavior?
3. What do you foresee happening if you do not change anything?
4. If change is needed, how committed are you to making it happen?

We are talking emotions here. Creation, implementation, and monitoring of a financial system starts thereafter.

So, you see emotions and how you manage those are the driving force of change.

Again, you have two choices.

1. Give in to the prevailing emotion of the moment. Your amygdala is dictating terms and you follow.

(The amygdala is a part of the brain involved with the experiencing of emotions)

2. Disagree with the prevailing emotion. Don't rationalize it. It opens up new avenues of thought.

Any number of listicles cannot help unless you go through this fundamental process.

We will see more real-life examples in our future discussions. Stay tuned.

KEY TAKEAWAYS

1. **Triggers for Change in Money Habits**

Problems or strong desires for improvement catalyze changes in money habits.

Change is initiated when a problem or strong desire rises to the conscious mind.

2. **Childhood Influence**

Financial sentiments formed at an early age become the basis for money habits.

3. **Adulthood and Overcoming Mistakes**

Many adults lack financial education from parents or teachers.

Adults often make mistakes in the early stages, requiring time to overcome.

4. **Money Management System**

A customized system, beyond Excel sheets and financial information, addresses established behavior and habits.

5. **Role of Emotions in Change**

Emotions drive change in money habits.

6. **Two choices**

Give in to the prevailing emotion dictated by the amygdala (brain region associated with emotions).

Disagree with the prevailing emotion, opening up new thought avenues.

CHAPTER 9

STRATEGIC SHIFTS – MASTERING THE ART OF CHANGING MONEY HABITS

Do we need to wait for that one life-changing incident, that makes a permanent change in our brain structure, and we are never the same again?

It may not happen. But the daily pains and struggles are real and speak of a need to change.

Have you ever been in any of these situations?

- You stay awake wondering how you will finance your child's education, your mother's treatment, or that dream house.
- You want to buy something. But you control the instinct and postpone the idea.
- You've read a book on wealth generation or the power of compounding and realize that you missed out on so many opportunities.
- You meet a friend after many years and admire the way he managed his money. You are inspired to do the same.
- You want to set an example for your children with positive money habits.

WHEEL OF LIFE

Needless to say, the goal needs to be clear. Let the destination recommend the path. The financial behavior being modeled to set an example for your children can be vastly different from saving money for a fancy car.

The Wheel of Life is a concept where you can write down the major areas of your life where you desire improvement.

Let us see an example below. This diagram shows the difference between where you are now, and where you would like to be. The numerical values are derived from the rating you give yourself on a scale of 1-10.

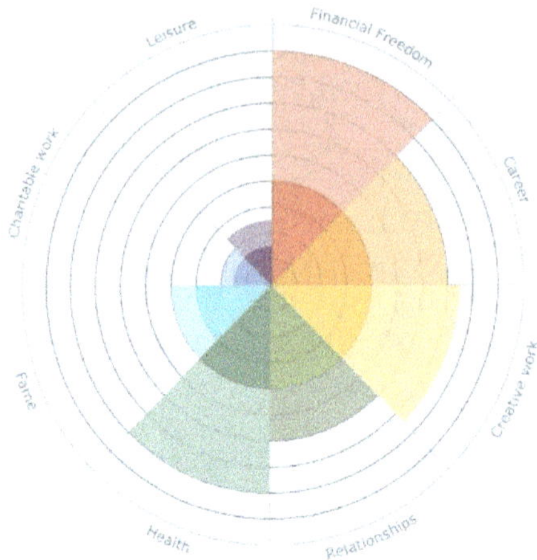

Life Domain	Now	Future	Gap
Relationships	4	10	6
Fame	2	8	6
Career	6	10	4
Charitable work	1	5	4
Creative work	7	10	3
Leisure	2	5	3
Health	8	10	2
Financial Freedom	10	10	0

It is not necessary that the desired rating in every sphere is 10. We are okay with a lesser rating in some areas, but we need to quantify it.

If you want relationships to be 10 but are presently on 4, the difference is 6.

If you want your career to be 10 but are presently on 6, the difference is 4.

You will be comfortable with leisure activities at 5, but it is languishing at a measly 2.

The higher the gap, more is the effort needed to inculcate the right habits to achieve the desired outcome.

CHANGE IS REPLACEMENT, NOT ELIMINATION

The mind can never be idle. Through meditation or creative visualization, one only replaces the negative with positive, the useless with productive, and the dormant with active thoughts.

The same applies to behavior or habits. **It is not enough to do or not do something**. The idea is to do the right things.

Jamie feels that he is spending too much money on transportation, but he cannot quit the job. He needs to go to work every day. Finding a job close to his house will help that may not always be a viable option.

What are the options?

- ☐ Can he switch to car-pooling, taking a comfortable AC bus or metro?
- ☐ Can he replace his car with a more fuel-efficient one?

Figuring out different options and giving them a try will take some time. He will get used to the new lifestyle at some point in time.

- ☐ Watching the savings accumulate in his bank account will encourage him to continue with it.
- ☐ The relief of not having a debt recovery agent remind him about missed EMIs will further cement the behavior.

In case there is a problem with the new option, and he has to switch back to driving alone, what is his Plan B?

- ☐ If he has been eating out for lunch, can he carry homemade food?
- ☐ Can he discontinue the subscriptions he is not using – like Netflix or the gym membership?

Needless to mention, Jamie may miss his companions from the carpool or metro and want to get back to the same routine again.

He chooses more than one option for saving money and manages to pay for his child's hobby classes. Watching the child blossom in his newfound talent is such a pleasure. It makes all the tweaks in a lifestyle look worthwhile.

Note that I refrain from using the word 'sacrifice' here. Sacrifice has negative connotations. You don't want to live with a crown of thorns and go down in history as the most unappreciated parent or spouse. You want to make happiness more inclusive and share it with everyone.

Jamie may need to let his family know about what he is doing. It will help them be careful with money, and devise new ways of maximizing wealth

LESSONS WE LEARN FROM JAMIE'S EXPERIENCE

- A change takes research and time. Don't expect overnight results.
- Rewards encourage behavior, till it becomes an entrenched habit. If I do something for 30-45 days continuously, I miss it on the 46th day. I want to keep doing it because it has become a part of my DNA.
- Track results. Check your savings account and loan account statements. If the changes look small in the beginning, remember what lessons on the power of compounding say – results are exponential towards the end.
- Reasonable can overtake rationale, as Morgan Housel says in his book "The Psychology of Money". We are not a spreadsheet, we are human beings – screwed up, emotional human beings.
- It does not mean that we never make a plan. It just means that we make a provision for diversions. Have a Plan B and Plan C. Invoke the backup plans only if needed. Even if you never have to do it, Plans B & C give a sense of comfort, that you have something to fall back on.

- Include your family or friends in your plan. Execution becomes easier when others do not pose a challenge to your efforts.

KEY TAKEAWAYS

1. Prompt Change

Change can be prompted by daily struggles or a desire for improvement.

2. Wheel of Life

The Wheel of Life concept helps quantify and prioritize desired improvements.

3. Replacement

Replacement, not elimination, is crucial for effective behavior change.

CHAPTER 10

NEUROSCIENCE OF WEALTH – PRIMING YOUR BRAIN FOR FINANCIAL SUCCESS

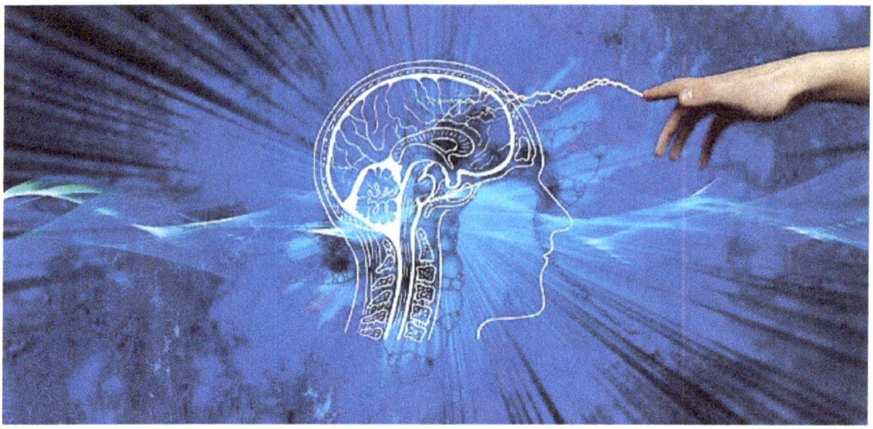

You watch videos and read listicles on good and bad money habits every day or every week. So much so, that you are likely to stop reading beyond a certain point because you know what to expect.

Your mind is bored of repetition, weary of information overdose, and hardwired enough to keep you where you are.

And this is where you fail to bring about change....

It's like you know smoking is bad for health but continue with it. Statutory warnings are everywhere in the fine print. The sellers are fulfilling a legal obligation. Why should it pull you out of your comfort zone?

THE BRAIN IS SUPER LAZY

So am I ... who are you to tell me that?

EHT NIARB SI REPUS YZAL

What the hell is happening here? I need to crack this puzzle.

What got you charged here? An unfamiliar set of alphabets put together weirdly arouses your curiosity.

Have you been feeding anything new to your tired brain?

Your thoughts become algorithms for the future.

If you come across something unfamiliar, you need new software to decode it, and you develop it in the neural pathways of your brain.

WHAT AM I SUPPOSED TO DO?

What did you do when you first learned how to read?

unseen nuances

call for attention, attract

untrained eyeballs

Does it pique your interest? Maybe, yes. Maybe you find it irrelevant to the topic. Hold on...

What happened when you learned to write? You learned to draw an image of the alphabet.

I learned to

hold tools the right way

draw a shape

meet the world

where language began

to start communicating

What has this got to do with Money or Money Habits?

See how money plays heavily on your mind – the riddle you cannot solve, the burden you want to shed, the Excel sheet that is not your style, the math you shunned from childhood.

- Start with something unrelated.
- Read a book in a different genre than your favorite ones.
- Play a different game with your child. Watch how he/she reacts, and watch how you change with his / her response.
- Visit websites different from the regular ones.

Your mind is priming for change.

Now, let's get down to money.

- Plan an outing in a nearby place of natural beauty on the weekend, rather than your weekly ritual of visiting the mall – to shop, watch your kid play a game you don't enjoy, and eat food cooked with standardized recipes.
- Learn a new recipe and cook. Watch your family appreciate or encourage you.
- Pull out all the clothes from your closet. Put them together in different ways to create new outfits. Invite ideas and opinions.
- Check out the AC bus service or metro, and commute without cursing other drivers in a traffic jam.

Did you enjoy it?

You've also saved money.

The idea is to trick your brain out of ingrained patterns, stop your hand from hitting the same buttons on devices, and rewire Habits (then, Money Habits)

> ***The mere exposure to things novel can be enough to have your brain automatically release the shackles of experience and make new judgments and connections.***
>
> **Henk from the Heart Math Institute**

I will let Henk summarize it for you.

- **Change your environment**
- **Make new acquaintances**
- **Seek new information and vantage points**

ALL THAT IS SAID ABOVE IS NOT ENOUGH

And now I add my two bits to it.

You don't have to believe what I say. I'm not one of those coaches who tell you,

"I did what my mentor asked me to do, and you need to do the same for success."

I learned things the hard way, but it was my way.

- Challenge every opinion and thought you come across. See what lies on the other side.
- Provoke your thought patterns. What would be the scenario if you tried something different?
- Compile conclusions that emerge. They need not match pre-existing patterns.
- Choose the best one to meet your goals.
- Be prepared to divert whenever you hit a roadblock. Adaptability is the key.

Money habits need not be a religion. But if they help you achieve what you want, unconsciously they become a religion.

KEY TAKEAWAYS

1. **Resistance to change**

Brain's resistance to change can be overcome by introducing novelty.

2. **Decoding Software**

Learning involves developing new decoding software in the brain.

3. **Priming the Mind**

Priming the mind for change involves starting with unrelated activities.

4. **Diversity**

Tricks for change include engaging in diverse activities to rewire habits.

5. **Novelty**

Exposure to novelty automatically releases the brain from experienced patterns.

CHAPTER 11

SECURING MONEY IS MORE IMPORTANT THAN SAVING

We focus on spending and saving while developing or reforming money habits. We learn about the right investments in money strategies. What we tend to ignore is that the conservation of financial assets we own is equally important.

Insurance is touted as the solution to all concerns about risk.

Undoubtedly, insurance is a strategy to compensate for the loss.

But we also need to develop safe habits, while doing our money transactions, to prevent loss.

DIGITAL MONEY

Let us accept that money is now digital. We need to accept the risks associated with digital transactions.

> ***"One of the main cyber-risks is to think they don't exist. The other is to try to treat all potential risks.***
>
> ***Fix the basics, protect first what matters for your business, and be ready to react properly to pertinent threats. Think data, but also business services integrity, awareness, customer experience, compliance, and reputation."***
>
> **Stephane Nappo**

Risk comes with the territory when you are breaking new ground. Learn how to evaluate and mitigate these risks rather than take away people's power and autonomy.

Leena Patel,

Raise Your Innovation IQ:
21 Ways to Think Differently
During Times of Change

HOW DO YOU KEEP YOUR MONEY SAFE?

Develop small habits that become part of your lifestyle. Don't feel humiliated by snide remarks on being over-cautious or paranoid.

1. **Let your money age. Spend it a certain number of days after receipt.**

It earns interest and over some time, gives compounding benefits.

2. **Before making an online payment or any financial transaction, switch the network from Wi-Fi to a mobile hotspot.**

It protects your data against being hacked.

3. **Delete all financial data such as SMS alerts, images of KYC, or other sensitive documents, immediately after having used those. You can keep those safe as attachments in email, to be downloaded as and when required.**

The apps on your phone cannot access the data. Be careful with Google Drive. Certain apps ask for permission to access your Google accounts, and data on the drive may not be safe.

4. **Delete all the apps that are not in use. You can download them again when needed.**

It prevents unnecessary leakage of data on your device.

5. **If the phone is overheated or the battery runs out rapidly with normal usage, get an anti-virus installed immediately. Check transactions in your bank and credit card accounts.**

It indicates that someone else has access to your phone.

6. **It is a good idea to let apps be updated, as the latest versions are designed to meet new challenges.**

Updates do occupy extra space, but you can counter it by deleting unnecessary files elsewhere.

7. **Change passwords regularly, even if the platform does not compel you to do so.**

Learn methods to generate passwords you can remember and are complex for a hacker at the same time.

8. **Set passwords for new platforms carefully.**

You need your email ID to sign up on a new platform. Ensure that you do not use your email password here. It protects your email account from being hacked.

9. **Have a separate email account for banking, insurance, and other investment platforms.**

Do not use this email id everywhere and let it become public.

10. **Check bank statements when received in the mail.**

Look out for unusual transactions that you are not aware of. It can be anything from charges being debited to money withdrawn from an ATM.

HOW DO YOU DEVELOP THE RIGHT MONEY MINDSET?

- **Think of alternates**

What will be the cost of buying the same thing or something that fulfills the same need from some other platform?

An iPad Mini gives me the benefit of a larger screen for reading books but cannot be used to make a phone call. Maybe a phone with a large screen is a better idea, than investing in two devices.

Is the same device available for rent? The model getting outdated will not affect me.

• Think of returns

An asset is something that can be converted to cash and/or generates an income for me.

A liability is something for which I incur a recurring cost, like a car or a rented house.

The difference should always be clear.

We should focus on increasing our net worth, instead of increasing income.

Net worth = Assets - Liabilities

We need to work for ourselves, not just for companies (utility bills and shopping), banks (loan installments, charges, and credit card bills), and real estate agents (commissions and rent).

• Think of the future cost

Buy Now Pay Later or swipe a credit card is easy.

How much more are you paying to buy on so-called easy installments?

How much more will you pay, if you fail to pay the full amount on the due date?

Debt drains future prosperity.

• Do everything in small measure

Deprivation leads to binges.

Spend on your passion, entertainment, and emotional needs to a predefined extent. If needed, compensate by cutting down something less important to you.

• Make your family a companion on your wealth journey

Share your ideas and plans with them. Inculcate a sense of anticipation or pride in what they will own at a later stage in life.

Enroll them in financial literacy courses if you feel they need input on money management.

Talk about money. Have a money conversation at least once a week.

KEY TAKEAWAYS

1. **Financial Conservation Focus**

While spending, saving, and investing are crucial, safeguarding financial assets through insurance and cultivating safe habits is equally vital.

2. **Digital Money Risks**

Recognizes the shift to digital currency and underscores the importance of understanding and mitigating associated risks in financial transactions.

3. **Safe Money Habits**

Recommends developing small, safety-oriented habits as part of daily life to protect against cyber threats, emphasizing data security, and efficient use of digital tools.

4. **Mindset for Financial Safety**

Encourages cultivating a money mindset that prioritizes security, including delaying spending, protecting personal data, and regularly updating passwords for online accounts.

5. **Family Involvement in the Wealth Journey**

Advocates for involving family members in financial discussions, educating them on money management, and fostering a collective understanding of financial goals for a secure and shared wealth journey.

CHAPTER 12

SIMPLIFIED STRATEGIES – FOUR ACES TO STREAMLINE MONEY HABITS

The habits that stick in the long run are the simplest ones.

A simple life is not seeing how little we can get by with—that's poverty—but how efficiently we can put first things first. When you're clear about your purpose and your priorities, you can painlessly discard whatever does not support these, whether it's clutter in your cabinets or

commitments on your calendar.

- Victoria Moran.

Reading books and learning online are good habits, but how much of the knowledge gained is imbibed into our lives?

Setting financial goals and finding the simplest way to reach them is undoubtedly the 20% effort that will deliver 80% of results.

Complexity is a cover to prevent people from reaching the truth. It is often used by celebrities to keep a mystique around themselves.

At home, the family will respectfully leave you alone if you talk about complex money management theories and investment strategies. They will ask for money to fulfill their needs and leave you alone with the rest.

THE ACE MAGIC

- ### Go by thumb rules.

Thumb rules are created to help easy adoption of complex principles.

Understand that these are not universally applicable and will not work in the same manner for all. Twist and turn to suit your needs, as you acquire financial sophistication.

Till then, the thumb rules keep you on the right track. It is like having a map or compass when you don't have GPRS on your phone.

- ### Don't always wait for the best

I'm always amused by certain questions on platforms like Quora, "Which is the best ...(plan, scheme, item, etc.) for ....?"

There is no best till I know your goals, resources, and risk appetite.

If you cannot afford a Lamborghini today, will you go without a car or buy something to suit your needs and budget? Let dreams continue to push you, but being on the road is important. Plans gain momentum only when they are already in action.

Don't let the lack of **best** become a hindrance to attaining **good**. Start with whatever is available.

• Take an annual view

Budgeting is a tool for anyone with finite resources and infinite wants. But budgets are often created weekly and monthly and block the annual or long-term view.

You know what your net take-home pay is and what are your monthly expenses.

What about the taxes, insurance premiums, and tax-saving investments?

What about the replacement of lost or damaged goods?

What about your annual holiday, weddings in the social sphere, or the trip taken to meet a family member who needs you?

The 20% or 30% you save cannot all go towards long-term retirement plans. You first need to put money aside for annual expenses, and then commit to other goals.

• Checklist of questions

You zero down on an investment plan and decide to put your money in it.

As we said above, it is important to start somewhere and not always wait for the best. However, since it is difficult to withdraw money from investment plans without incurring a loss, you must have a basic checklist before committing.

See if you can tick at least 80%-90% of the boxes, before saying **I do**.

The first set of questions should be about how it meets your financial goals within the existing resources.

The second set will be about what the investment plan gives you.

The third is to know the actual returns after deducting costs. You must know all kinds of fees, charges, and penalties levied by the company you are investing in, to avoid unpleasant surprises.

MODALITIES AND SUB-MODALITIES

Modalities are methodologies of doing things. You have a goal. You make a plan by figuring out the best route to reach there. You start acting on it.

Sub-modalities are the little things you do every day, every week to keep up the momentum.

Money habits for success and all that we have discussed are these sub-modalities.

What spurs you on? Of course, everybody identifies and adopts it.

What stops you from being on the desired path? You must know this and work at eliminating the blocks to succeed.

Spending habits, saving habits, entertaining habits, money consumption habits, communication habits, and relationships all become the sub-modalities to become Smart Money Habits.

KEY TAKEAWAYS

1. **Simplicity Wins:** Embrace simple habits aligned with your purpose to efficiently manage both life and finances.
2. **ACE Approach:** Follow the ACE magic – Go by thumb rules, Start with what's available, and Take an annual view for practical financial decision-making.
3. **Action Over Perfection:** Begin with accessible options rather than waiting for the elusive "best," as progress is born from taking initiative.
4. **Comprehensive Planning:** Look beyond monthly budgets, considering annual factors like taxes, insurance, and major life events for a holistic financial strategy.
5. **Checklist Discipline:** Before committing to investments, use a checklist to ensure alignment with goals, understand returns, and be aware of all associated costs for informed decision-making.
6. Monitoring progress from plan to implementation is crucial for success.

CHAPTER 13

CRUCIAL INSIGHTS – LONG AND SHORT OF MONEY HABITS

How many books on investor behavior have you read so far?

I can recommend a few outright

1. Behaviour Gap, by Carl Richards
2. Psychology of Money – by Morgan Housel
3. Same as Ever – by Morgan Housel
4. The Compound Effect – by Darren Hardy
5. The Millionaire Mind – by Thomas J. Stanley

The common thread running through all the books is about

1. Keep your focus on the long term, and not getting waylaid by short-term developments.
2. Stay focused on your life goals rather than the economy or something you cannot change.

Where do habits fall in the picture?

Habits are short-term acts, that help in retaining control of long-term goals.

It is what I can do today.

Then why is it so difficult to form money habits and stick to those?

Is it that we don't know what to do? **We know**. We are being bombarded with information from all sides.

We may not know what to choose. And that is because you are not clear about your goals.

We treat money habits like New Year resolutions that do not last beyond the first three weeks of January.

What stops us?

1. Lack of faith

What's the point? I'm going to fail anyway.

2. Rationalizing

Skipping it once won't make much of a difference. The amount is so miniscule anyway.

3. Avoidance

It's overwhelming. I can't be counting beans all my life. I'm not cut out for this.

4. Fear of being judged

What will they think about me (repeating clothes, driving an old car, not giving an expensive gift)? I can't explain my financial compulsions to the whole world.

5. Defensiveness

I can't help it. Unexpected guests will arrive. My kid always finds something new in the market that s/he can't do without. My wife will never stop shopping for things not needed.

HOW TO STOP NEGATIVE THOUGHTS?

I know a couple who never let me complete a sentence if it brings up an idea that seems alien to them. The immediate response is

"We don't do that or believe in it.

We have never done it."

And they haven't even heard what I have to say. It isn't very pleasant.

But the one thing I learned about them is that they have a very strongly defined self, and they don't let anyone or anything change it. Their self-perception is aligned with whatever they wish to achieve, and they can firmly stay on the path.

What was it that got them on this defensive path? I don't know. But at some point, they must have felt a need to protect their interests against outside influence. It is this realization that removes guilt or shame from the picture. You know that you are doing things in a certain way in your best interest.

There is a process of observing, learning, sorting out what you need from the sphere of influence, and then firmly sticking to the chosen path.

Yes, a review is needed. But only when circumstances change. Otherwise, the positive results (however small) should keep you firmly on track.

WHAT DO YOU NEED TO TELL YOURSELF?

I value myself, and I won't be at anybody's mercy in times of need.

I don't know or don't care about what others think. I'll give it a try.

I will put in my best effort and get the best results.

If others are using my resources, they need to respect my decisions about it. Peace in relationships is not a one-sided process.

Life is short, and I can't afford to fail on my expectations.

I cannot keep everyone happy, so I might as well please myself.

FOUR QUESTIONS TO ASK YOURSELF

1. What will I gain if I succeed?
2. What will I lose if I succeed?
3. What will I gain if I fail?
4. What will I lose if I fail?

All your motivation and conclusions lie within the boundaries of the answers.

KEY TAKEAWAYS

1. **Long-Term Focus**

Maintain focus on long-term financial goals, avoiding distraction from short-term developments or external factors beyond control.

2. **Habits as Control**

Recognize habits as short-term actions crucial for retaining control over long-term financial objectives.

3. **Challenges in Habit Formation**

Overcome challenges in forming money habits, including lack of faith, rationalization, avoidance, fear of judgment, and defensiveness.

4. **Mindset Shift**

Shift mindset by valuing oneself, disregarding external opinions, and staying on the chosen financial path for personal satisfaction.

5. **Self-Reflection Questions**

Ask critical self-reflection questions to uncover motivations, emphasizing gains and losses associated with both success and failure.

CHAPTER 14

CONQUERING CHALLENGES TO FORM NEW HABITS

We suffer from information overload. So, most of us know what are the ideal behavior patterns, the new habits we need to inculcate, and the things we need to give up to reach our desired goals. Facebook, WhatsApp, LinkedIn, and other social media channels work untiringly to bring this information to us.

However, research shows that very few of our lofty New Year resolutions last beyond the 17th of January.

What stops us?

What makes us slip back into an old behavior pattern, when we know and accept that we need to change?

HABIT BLOCKERS

☐ Identity

A new habit compels us to change our identity, and our old self resists that.

Our social circle knows us as someone who dresses in expensive brands, drives a particular car, and always holidays abroad. It is difficult to break that identity and grow into a new one.

Everybody tells you about the Power of Habit – how it becomes your character, personality, or destiny. Nobody tells you about that one mindset that creates habit.

It is not an addiction. It is not a compulsion. It is not inheritance.

It is a sense of pride in being different. It is self-glorification in doing something. It is a crutch used to boost self-esteem. It gets interlinked to identity – Aisa hi hoon main (This is how I am........) How often do we hear the following?

I just can't eat cabbage (or anything healthy but considered low-brow or commonplace)

I cannot sleep before 2 am (No effort has been made to do that. A different lifestyle sets one apart)

I love caviar (My neighbors can't afford it)

A habit will not change, as long as one takes pride in it. The subconscious keeps pushing one towards it. There is resistance to enforced change, as it hurts self-esteem. Take pride in a new habit, and it gets ingrained in the personality.

I am cost-conscious. (though I can afford to spend more)

I am health conscious (though I can afford to eat out every day)

Change the conversation with yourself. Life will change.

The reverse is equally true. It is not always about being less than what we are now. We are hesitant to face the world being more efficient, attractive, or richer than we have been. There is a hidden fear of sarcastic comments – *"Oh, you? Couldn't recognize..."*

We've discussed this in a previous chapter. The way out is to change the identity internally. We need to see and accept ourselves as what we intend to be in the future, for our good.

☐ Mind

The mind seeks immediate gratification.

We love that compliment, our beautiful image in the mirror, or the high that we get from certain things.

We cannot miss out on that to get into the garb of a new self.

Here we can set reminders everywhere of where we would like to be.

It is cliched to say hang a beautiful dress in a smaller size near the dresser, to inspire weight loss. But something similar like checking your financial statements or reducing monthly bills can be helpful. The fact that you paid all your dues in time and yet have a surplus left is exhilarating. Closure of loan accounts vindicates all your efforts and more than compensates for delaying gratification.

☐ Body

The body resists change.

The feeling of being in your car or cab is very different from that of being in public transport. People getting back to work after the pandemic feel uncomfortable in formal attire, even though they've lived in those clothes for decades before.

The traveling business class certainly feels better than the economy or a train.

Children who refuse to eat certain things have never tasted them. They are comfortable with a familiar dinner plate. You just need to introduce them to different cuisines to broad-base the palate.

Similarly, we need to get the body to experience different facets, till it all feels normal.

☐ Beliefs

We have internal set points for whatever we do. We've defined our boundary lines and caged ourselves. There is a strong internal resistance to crossing those lines.

We must help family members financially if we earn more than them.

Gifting at a certain level is a social norm we need to abide by.

A particular brand is good for us, despite the market being flooded with many more options.

A child of this family needs to be a doctor/lawyer/chartered accountant or whatever

These are examples of internal set points.

The only way out is to build new set points. But how do we do this?

We interact more with people from other belief systems to widen our perspective. You may not know of new-age career options till a career counselor tells you about them.

We read publications and visit websites other than the ones we regularly track.

Be the Devil's Advocate and challenge your own belief from the other side of the fence. You believe that a certain thing is true, but what happens if it turns out to be false? How will you position yourself at that point?

☐ Emotions

The problem with the stock market and emotions is volatility, though they are both essential and intrinsic to the systems they are part of.

A trigger shifts your emotional state, and then you react to the new emotional state.

Somebody challenges your status, and you are out to prove them wrong. Of course, you can afford to buy X or do Y stuff. Multi-level marketing professionals use this to the hilt.

A person from a less privileged background invokes pity and you go out of your way to help them. NGOs and crowd-funding ads exploit this mindset by posting pictures of pain and pathos.

The remedy is to identify the trigger and stop there. Being aware helps. It stops you on the track before you veer off your path to a goal.

☐ Desire for freedom

We want the freedom to disengage from something when we want. So a commitment of any kind is anathema.

We say that we don't like slavery, not realizing that this voice emanates from another deep-rooted slave mindset that resists change.

Someone sells us a subscription saying that we are free to cancel it at any point. We like that but fail to see other terms and conditions like a higher initial cost or a penalty later to avail of this freedom.

Freedom is the ability to opt for Plan B if Plan A does not work. It is the relief you feel in the end after a certain goal is accomplished.

Spending less is painful. But let us be clear that new desired money habits are not always about spending less.

At times, spending more now may save money in the long run. It can be a discount on a long-term description, a high-quality product that lasts longer, or an investment in a club membership that helps you get more business.

The propensity to save money now can go against us if we do not keep the long-term picture in mind.

So, the idea is to reach an optimal scale, not a minimal one. Alignment to self-defined goals is more important than your public persona or an imposed value system.

KEY TAKEAWAYS

1. **Identity Alignment**

Acknowledge the resistance to changing habits linked to identity. Embrace pride in new habits, as self-glorification aligns with the desired changes.

2. **Mind's Immediate Gratification**

Counter the mind's pursuit of immediate gratification by setting reminders for long-term goals. Celebrate financial achievements and closure of loans to reinforce delayed gratification.

3. **Body's Resistance to Change**

Address the body's resistance to change by gradually exposing it to different experiences. Make unfamiliar financial habits feel normal, akin to introducing diverse cuisines to broaden the palate.

4. **Challenging Internal Beliefs**

Challenge internal set points and beliefs by interacting with diverse perspectives, exploring alternative career options, reading different publications, and playing the Devil's Advocate to test existing beliefs.

5. **Emotional Awareness**

Recognize triggers that shift emotional states, especially in financial decisions. Being aware of emotional responses helps prevent veering off the path to financial goals.

6. **Desire for Freedom**

Understand the desire for freedom and commitment aversion. Realize that financial habits aren't always about spending less; optimal scale and alignment with self-defined goals take precedence over imposed values.

CHAPTER 15

BLIND SPOTS EXPOSED – ENHANCING MONEY MANAGEMENT SKILLS

You cannot see your back, but you can feel an itch.

There are parts of your psyche, which you can neither see nor feel. Those may still have an impact on others or your life.

Have you heard of the Johari Window?

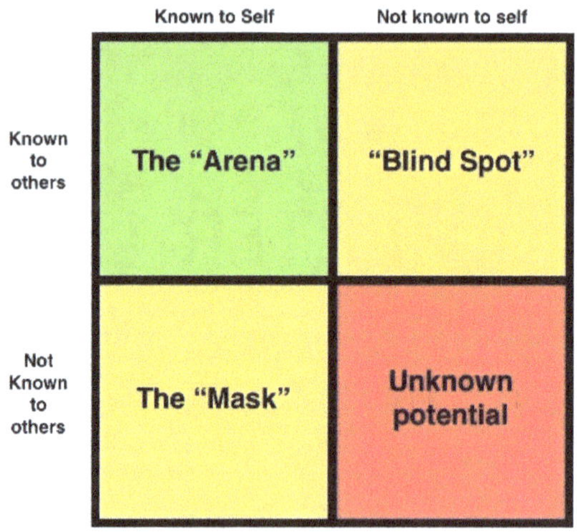

Johari Window

If you write an autobiography, you'll focus on the Arena – parts of your life known to yourself and others. Then, you may sprinkle it with some facts not known to others. It arouses curiosity and increases excitement. It also gives you the pleasure of having a good strategy in place, of achieving what you want without revealing too much.

The people who know you might have a different story to tell. Your book will be discussed in drawing room conversations "But who will tell him that ....?"

Do you recall an old hit movie "Khubsoorat" starring Rekha? The matriarch of the family is known for her harsh discipline. At a certain point, she is confronted by the truth that the family abides by her imposed discipline out of fear and helplessness, not love. She is heartbroken and says certain things would have gone wrong, in the absence of the rules she set. She had **blind spots**, or was wearing a **mask** as a strategy?

WHAT ARE BLIND SPOTS?

These are the areas you ignore while making a decision. The reason is any kind of bias, belief, or fear – recency bias, confirmation bias, a strongly held belief that may not be close to reality, or a deeply ingrained fear that prevents sound decision-making.

Where do you see yourself in the picture, when you manage money?

What goes through your mind when you decide to buy a new house or car or splurge on a beautiful, luxury item? Are you reveling in the sense of comfort, the compliments you'll be showered with?

Do you see the bills, interest to be paid, and the long-term opportunity cost of money spent now?

COMMON BLIND SPOTS

- **Opportunity cost**

This is a very common blind spot. We are unable to see alternate and better ways of utilizing the same amount.

- **Tradition**

We believe that our children will look after us in the same manner that we have looked after our parents. Or do you believe that they will look after you because you've been a better parent than the ones you had?

- **Blind trust**

We trust people because we've never cheated on anyone, and we expect others to be like us.

- **Historical performance**

Every seller of market-related financial products shows you historical data because they do not know the future. Nor do you. Yet, you decide to go with it in the absence of an alternative. The future is only imagination. The element of uncertainty will always remain.

Yet, you are not emotionally stable when confronted by a loss. Deep down, you believed that the trends would continue in the same way.

- **Assumption of continuity**

You will never take a loan swipe a credit card or use Buy Now Pay Later schemes if you believe that your income will not continue at the same level or grow in the future.

At the same time, does it hurt to borrow a little less than what you think you can repay?

ADJUST THE MIRROR TO CHECK YOUR BLIND SPOTS

How do you manage to check your blind spots while driving?

If the rearview mirror reflects the side of your car, it is of no help. You know where the side of your car is because you are sitting in it.

The mirror should be positioned to reflect other vehicles from behind. This is what always keeps you in control.

Apply the metaphor to your life.

How to reduce blind spots?

Re-adjust the mirror to see what's happening on the road, rather than the side of your car.

Lean your face against the glass.

Look left. Look right.

All I mean to say is to seek different opinions. Talk to people who hold views different from yours. Try to see things from their perspective. Maybe you see merit in it.

Blind spots and biases are closely followed by blind spots and rationalization. We find every possible reason to justify our decisions. Meanwhile, truth falls in the gaps.

The biggest barrier to brainstorming is that the participants think their ideas might be odd or irrelevant. But when expressed, one of them leads to success.

We do this to ourselves all the time. We refuse to entertain certain thoughts because they appear irrelevant. Your image, your self-esteem, and your expectations of your social circle show you a certain mirror that gives only a partial view.

There is no harm in listening – in water cooler chats, on social media, and in articles that your least favorite authors write.

Listen to feedback, and not always from people you like and trust.

There is a beacon of light somewhere, that you refuse to acknowledge.

Many financial planning experts hand over their money to others to manage.

This comes from a retired investment banker

> ***"I could manage my own money, except for the 'I' part."***

We hire a coach because s/he is not us. It adds value.

And coming back to Johari's window.

We've not spoken about Potential as yet, the part that is unknown to us and unknown to others.

It spells hope that there is still a better way out. We have it in us to change for good. Optimal utilization of potential will define your future.

KEY TAKEAWAYS

1. Johari Window Awareness

Recognize the Johari Window concept – the parts of your life known to yourself and others, and those unknown. Blind spots are areas you ignore due to biases, beliefs, or fears.

2. Common Blind Spots

Identify common blind spots, including overlooking opportunity costs, relying on traditions, blind trust, historical performance assumptions, and the assumption of continuity in income.

3. Adjust the Mirror

Adjust your metaphorical mirror to reduce blind spots. Seek different opinions, consider diverse perspectives, and be open to ideas that challenge your own. Embrace feedback, even from sources you may not initially trust.

4. Rationalization Awareness

Be mindful of biases and rationalization, as they can obstruct objective decision-making. Embrace diverse thoughts, as odd or irrelevant ideas might lead to successful outcomes.

5. Unlocking Potential

Embrace the unknown potential (Johari Window's "Potential" quadrant) as a source of hope and opportunity. Acknowledge the possibility of change for the better and optimal utilization of untapped potential to define your future.

CHAPTER 16

DEBT MASTERY-CULTIVATING MONEY HABITS TO MANAGE DEBT

The home loan market has expanded in the last few years. Affordable housing schemes, low-interest rates, and the need for more space in work-from-home scenarios all contributed to the rise.

Now comes another rise to contend with – a rise in interest rates.

EMIs are set to increase and create pressure on household budgets.

What are the new money habits needed to manage debt well, in case you are affected by the hike?

It is not necessary to reach a debt-zero situation. Debt habits need to change for better debt management.

How debt affects mental health is another point to be considered. Hence, the need for better money habits cannot be over-emphasized.

WHY DEBT MANAGEMENT IS IMPORTANT WHEN INTEREST RATES RISE

BNPL Schemes

Start small.

How many BNPL schemes are you enrolled in, because you clicked on an available option while paying?

No interest is indeed charged if you pay the bill on time. However, too many loan accounts leave an adverse impact on your credit score.

You are likely to miss a due date if there are too many bills to be paid.

Companies offering BNPL schemes are folding up because they failed to recover money. It means people borrow more than what they can afford or are wilful defaulters. If the situation is bad for the lenders, it is worse for borrowers. Their credit scores are adversely impacted by failure to repay minuscule amounts.

Credit cards

Keep your credit cards if there are no annual charges. Use a little money from all cards, so that you don't max out any.

Ensure that the percentage utilization of available credit limits is low. Credit utilization Ratio is the proportion of available limits that you use. The lower the CUR, the higher your credit score.

Don't cancel credit cards because it will reduce the overall credit limit. Consequently, the percentage utilization will increase with the same amount of expenditure.

Needless to say, pay the full amount on the due date. Automate bill payments, so that you don't inadvertently miss a payment. Do not fall prey to the Minimum Amount Due to syndrome. It will land you deeper in debt.

Budgeting

Budgeting is imperative if increased loan installments are creating pressure.

Use a diary, an Excel sheet, or a budgeting app whatever is convenient.

Sticking to the budget may overrule the purchase of new assets or indulge in impulse buying.

A lower budget may imply changing means of transport, eating out habits, annual subscriptions, or a reduction in holiday or entertainment expenses. **It will need a change of mindset and new habits.**

1. Automate all bill payments

This will ensure that you do not pay any penalty for a late payment.

2. Create an emergency fund

An emergency fund prevents straying from the budget, or leakage of money from long--

3. Evaluate balance transfers

Check fixed rate options in a rising interest rate regime.

But be aware that it binds you for a long time. What if the floating rate next year is less than the fixed rate you opted for? Pre-closure of a fixed-rate loan attracts charges, so it will restrict options for further balance transfers.

There is no one-size-fits-all solution. So, options need to be evaluated as per the amount of debt you owe, the rate of interest, your age, and household income.

4. Be careful in availing of fresh loans

Stay away from credit card debt and personal loans.

If you need money, look at gold loans, top-up in-home loans, or loans against property which are comparatively cheap.

5. Settle some debts with full payment

You may choose to settle the small amounts first or the loans with the highest rate of interest. It depends on how much money can you spare.

6. Make prepayment a habit

Use all additional inflows such as a performance increment, bonus, incentive, or a large windfall in business to prepay a certain amount of debt.

It keeps the interest burden low in the long run.

Decide wisely which debt to settle first.

7. Rebalance your investment portfolio

Check the real rate of return on investments. It means that investments should yield returns higher than the interest you are paying to combat inflation.

If this is not the case, you need to reallocate funds to stay afloat in the long run.

8. Review financial goals

Maybe you have to wait longer to buy a second home or something else you had planned for.

You need to plan how to manage within existing means.

If you are stopping a SIP to pay the increased EMI, it will affect your long-term financial goals. Check the time in which you can get back or track, or if you can compensate for that by generating a higher return somewhere else.

FD rates will also increase along with your EMIs. Closing FDs running at lower rates and booking them again at the highest rate for a longer term will help in the long run.

KEY TAKEAWAYS

1. BNPL Scheme Caution

Exercise caution with Buy Now Pay Later (BNPL) schemes to prevent credit score impact and missed payments.

2. Credit Card Wisdom

Keep credit cards with no annual fees, use them moderately, and avoid canceling to maintain credit limits.

3. Budgeting for Stability

Implement budgeting tools to manage increased loan installments, necessitating potential changes in spending habits.

4. Financial Automation

Automate bill payments and establish an emergency fund to maintain financial stability and prevent late fees.

5. Debt Management Tactics

Prioritize settling debts, evaluate balance transfers, and exercise caution with new loans to adapt to rising interest rates effectively.

CHAPTER 17

EASTERN WISDOM – UNLOCKING JAPANESE MONEY HABITS

A survey of the Japanese scene won't show it as a very conservative society. They hunger for luxury items and electronic gadgets, pay a premium for rare objects seen as status symbols, and are careful about how they dress and look.

However, the Japanese can be differentiated from others in two ways

1. **Connectedness to roots and heritage**
2. **Mindfulness**

New entrants to Japan are astonished by the way locals discard used stuff on the streets. There is no market for preloved goods. Is it a sign of prosperity, or insouciant wastage?

A possible reason could be the availability of new goods at affordable costs, and hence, unwillingness to pay for used goods. Or it could be their way of striking a social balance – letting the needy find something worthwhile without having to beg for it.

HERITAGE

The Japanese money management system is called Kakeibo.

Indians have traditionally had their ' bahi-khatas' (ledgers) for business and 'hisab ki diary' maintained by our parents and grandparents. However, it was a method for recording expenditure and gave a post-event view.

Kakeibo starts with the same concept – just record all items of income and expenses for some time. Expenses are divided into four categories – needs, wants, culture (entertainment), and unforeseen expenses.

The method extends further to conscious spending.

- Write down your goals.
- Decide on a savings goal.
- **Apply thought before spending money. Are you in sync with your goals?**

There is a financially aware section of youngsters who choose to **spend time to save money, rather than spend money to save time.**

Doesn't the latter summarize all our so-called convenience expenses?

There are soft copies and electronic versions of Kakeibo available, but the original Japanese method is to write in a notebook by hand. They believe that writing by hand connects the mind to the word better, and people are more likely to follow the rules.

It allows reflecting and acting.

KAIZEN AND MINDFULNESS

Kaizen is the art and science of making small improvements to overcome habits.

The human mind suffers from a negative bias. We believe in the negative easily and give in to fears and insecurities. Hope and positivity seem less real. Marketers take advantage of this propensity to induce spending. They exploit insecurity and the need for social acceptability. They induce FOMO (fear of missing out) to get those bucks out of your wallet.

One can overcome this bias by inducing mindfulness.

Do you seek relief from stress and boredom by spending money on food or clothes? Most of us do.

How does one overcome the temptation to spend money online,

on things you don't need?

- ☐ *Think about what you were thinking when you bought it.*
- ☐ *The sale ends at midnight today, and I won't get this fantastic price tomorrow.*
- ☐ *I need to have something new to show when we have visitors.*
- ☐ *My friends will envy me for sure.*
- ☐ *I must compensate my family for spending less time with them.*
- ☐ *We are social beings and certain things need to be done to keep up with others.*

What you should have been thinking?

- ☐ *Do I have something in my wardrobe to team this up with?*
- ☐ *Where will this item be languishing after a month or year?*
- ☐ *Can I buy this just when I need it? Sale prices are deceptive.*
- ☐ *Can this amount be put to better use?*
- ☐ *Am I sacrificing a long-term goal to indulge in this whim right now?*

How do I feel after buying this?

- ☐ *I must hide this somewhere.*
- ☐ *I regret being carried away by ....*
- ☐ *Am I being responsible ethically and sustainably?*
- ☐ *Can I buy peace or happiness with money?*
- ☐ *Is it a reprieve from some problem?*

I strongly recommend the book "Kaizen – the Japanese Method for Transforming Habits, One Step at a Time" By Sarah Harvey. It helps debug your mindset.

KEY TAKEAWAYS

1. **Kakeibo Money Management**

Kakeibo is the Japanese money management system.
It involves recording income and expenses, and categorizing them into needs, wants, culture, and unforeseen expenses.
Encourages conscious spending, setting goals, and saving with handwritten reflection.

2. **Kaizen for Mindfulness**

Kaizen focuses on making small improvements to overcome habits.
Combat negative biases by inducing mindfulness in spending decisions.
Reflect on thoughts behind purchases, avoid FOMO, and question the true value of the expenditure.

3. **Handwritten Connection**

Original Kakeibo emphasizes writing by hand in a notebook for a stronger mind-word connection.
The act of physically writing is believed to enhance mindfulness, reflection, and adherence to financial rules.

4. **Overcoming Temptations**

Identify and challenge common thoughts driving impulsive spending.
Consider the long-term consequences and sacrifice of goals for momentary whims.
Reflect on ethical and sustainable aspects of purchases for responsible spending.

5. **Resource Recommendation**

The book "Kaizen – the Japanese Method for Transforming Habits, One Step at a Time" by Sarah Harvey is suggested for mindset debugging and habit transformation.

CHAPTER 18

THE PSYCHOLOGY BEHIND FINANCIAL PLANNER AVOIDANCE

Financial planning is 90% mindset and 10% technique. Financial wellness is a 100% mindset.

The feeling of being comfortable with your money situation is priceless. It eliminates the root cause of many other conflicts in life.

ARE FINANCIAL PLANNERS WORTH IT?

But many of us avoid meeting a financial planner – for weeks, months, and years – at least for the first time.

The nagging thoughts are

- I've not been on the right track, and I'll look like a fool.
- Gathering all financial details will take a lot of time.
- I can't share all personal concerns and family conflicts with an outsider
- I don't want to be bound by a plan. I want my freedom to spend or give.
- How much will he charge?
- The advice may be biased in favor of the products they endorse.
- Do they have a minimum income or minimum corpus norm? Will I fit into that?
- I need money outside the investible corpus, where the financial planner cannot dictate terms.
- Bean counters working on Excel sheets don't understand the emotional and relationship complexities we function in.
- They'll be judgemental about the investments I've already made.

Financial planners do ask for a lot of details

1. Financial goals
2. Risk appetite
3. Risk coverage
4. Monthly expenses
5. Time horizons
6. Expected rate of return
7. How much can you afford to lose in a market crash?

Let us deal with the psychological discomfort first.

WHAT WE DON'T WANT TO ADMIT

The information we hide from others and sometimes ourselves is our expenditure on 'wants'.

What others see as 'wants' may be 'essential' for us, because of the psychological comfort it gives. We are addicted to lifestyles and do not wish to dilute. Clothes, accessories, cigarettes, alcohol, eating out, beauty salons, holidays are all a part of it. Someone in the family circle does not approve of your so-called fetishes.

So, you hide the information in whatever manner you can. I know women who hide the 46th pair of shoes or the twenty-fifth handbag they bought today. Guys may flaunt a Blue Label amongst their friends, but not look in the wife's eye while placing it in the bar.

And talking about it to a rank outsider is scary.

WHAT WE DON'T WANT TO FACE

Sujay met a financial planner (FP) for the first time with the following numbers

- Financial goals
- Minimum monthly expenses
- Time horizons

It turned out that the amount he saved was not enough to meet financial goals in the desired time frame. The only way out was to cut down on expenses. Now, this is bitter medicine.

The FP's face looked like that of a doctor, putting him on a strict diet.

WHAT WE DON'T WANT TO REVEAL

Financial goals do not materialize in thin air. They reflect the state of our relationships, individual priorities, and a deep-seated value system.

Rachna wants a house of her own before they have a baby. However, revealing this will create friction in the joint family where she lives now. She is not sure if her husband will stand by her, so she has never broached the topic with him.

She fears a concrete investment plan, as her preferences will be out in the open. What if the discord becomes too much to handle, and she wants to roll back her dreams?

Yet, the yearning for her dream nest continues to haunt her. She stacks up money in her VPF and bank deposits but is not sure how will it help.

WHAT CAN BE DONE?

Take one small bite at a time.

If you need to collect financial details, do the insurance part this month, and bank statements and loan accounts in another. In 3-6 months, you will have the data in one place. It will be the foundation stone of your financial plan.

If you need to talk about something, start dropping hints. Narrate the stories of friends and relatives. Talk about your childhood and what drives you to spend more or less now. It will prepare the ground for much-needed conversations.

If you know what should be done but tend to do something else, engage a financial coach. A financial coach is a coach with a background in personal finance. S/he will help you move certain things from the subconscious to the conscious level. Knowing the problem helps you decide what to do with it.

The financial coach can help you in devising a financial plan without recommending specific products or selling anything.

We'll talk more about the role of a financial coach in the next chapter.

KEY TAKEAWAYS

1. **Mindset Matters**

Financial planning is a 90% mindset, emphasizing the critical role of a positive and proactive financial mindset.

2. **Comfort is Priceless**

Achieving a state of comfort with one's financial situation is invaluable, in resolving underlying conflicts in life.

3. **Hesitations with Planners**

Common hesitations include fear of judgment, privacy concerns, and uncertainty about fees when considering financial planners.

4. **Detailed Information Required**

Financial planners need various details like goals, risk appetite, expenses, and time horizons to create effective plans.

5. **Challenges to Overcome**

Overcoming discomfort with revealing 'wants,' facing financial truths, and addressing underlying relationship dynamics are essential steps in financial planning.

CHAPTER 19

FINANCIAL COACHING UNVEILED

Money does not dictate your lifestyle. It's what you do to get it and how you manage your finances that determine your lifestyle.

Wayne Chirisa

Most of us in India cannot differentiate between a financial advisor and a financial coach.

The entities we commonly deal with are fee-only financial

planners, financial advisors, or mutual funds distributors. Some of us plan our investment strategies based on free advice doled out in social media groups or investing apps.

Some have moved a notch ahead and undertaken financial literacy courses.

Yet, none of these resources address your mental, emotional, and financial needs at the same time. We have an Excel sheet with a plan but are unable to adhere to it.

Procrastination is the rebellion of the soul against entrapment.

And why does the soul feel trapped? There is something in the plan that does not go with our psychological needs. There is a mental block you are unable to explain. There is a family problem you are unable to share.

Forming the right money habits is what we talk about in this series, but which habits are right for you? Is there a way to meet your financial goals, without moving a mountain?

Money and relationships are the most confidential part of an individual's life. We hear more about relationship problems being discussed than money problems in public.

WHO NEEDS A FINANCIAL COACH?

All of us know people who

- struggle with managing money after losing an

earning member of the family
- struggle with adhering to a budget or investment plan
- regret the emotional decisions they take regarding investments
- are burdened with debt
- want to plan their lifestyle or retirement in line with their passion and value system
- strive for financial wellness rather than a high net worth
- suffer from a shopping addiction
- are unable to say No when others ask for help

WHO IS A FINANCIAL COACH?

A financial coach is a non-judgmental companion to help you on the path to financial wellness. S/he is a certified life coach with a background in personal finance.

WHAT DOES A FINANCIAL COACH DO?

They ask you to state your problem or desired outcome as you see it.

Then, they lead you to view the actual situation through a series of questions and a heart-to-heart conversation. The coach is non-judgmental and just gives a direction to your thought process.

The real source of the problem may lie elsewhere than the place you perceive it.

The financial coach will then give you exercises, activities, and questionnaires to help you figure out where you are and where you want to reach.

Now, comes the second part of devising a plan to meet your financial goals.

You chunk your goals into smaller parts and make a step-by-step weekly fortnightly or monthly plan. This could be a budget or a conversation you need to have with stakeholders in your life.

The coach is there to handhold and monitor your progress. S/he follows through with your progress and helps you get back on track if you falter.

The entire exercise is done through face-to-face interactions in person, on the phone, or through video conferencing as per your comfort level. I know people who are more comfortable talking on the phone when they are not being watched.

The exercises and questionnaires can be delivered through email or any other mode of communication.

We advise an engagement of 6-12 months, with fortnightly or monthly interactions.

ARE FINANCIAL COACHES WORTH IT?

A financial coach solves a problem at the root.

Financial coaching helps you integrate the financial plan with your personality, such that it becomes a lifestyle rather than a task to be executed.

In case of a stubborn mental block, sessions with a hypnotherapist can be arranged.

KEY TAKEAWAYS

1. **Money and Lifestyle**

Your lifestyle isn't dictated by money itself, but by how you earn it and manage your finances, shaping the way you live.

2. **Role Confusion**

Many individuals in India often confuse financial advisors, financial planners, and mutual funds distributors. Differentiating among these roles is crucial for effective financial management.

3. **Addressing Mental and Emotional Needs**

Common financial resources, like fee-only financial planners or advisors, may not address mental, emotional, and financial needs simultaneously. Procrastination often stems from a lack of alignment between financial plans and psychological needs.

4. **The Rebellion of Procrastination**

Procrastination is described as the soul's rebellion against feeling trapped. Understanding the psychological aspects of financial planning is essential for overcoming procrastination and implementing effective strategies.

5. **The Role of a Financial Coach**

A financial coach is a certified life coach with a background in personal finance, offering non-judgmental support. They assist individuals in articulating their financial challenges, addressing mental blocks, and devising personalized plans aligned with their personalities and lifestyles.

CHAPTER 20

TOTAL MASTERY: DOMINATING YOUR MONEY HABITS FOR LASTING SUCCESS

Money habits are the total of our personality and upbringing. The upbringing reflects your parents' experience.

The evolution of money and how we hold it makes a lot of difference. Once upon a time, wealth in the form of gold, silver, and jewels was stashed away in guarded vaults or buried in metal pots. It was not easy to squander it without the knowledge of co-owners or family.

Paper money personalized ownership as we carry it in our pockets.

Digital money lives in our phones and facilitates both spending and overspending. At the same time, the right app can help you stay in control without checking too many bank statements or balancing the checkbook.

The concept of investing expanded from real estate and gold to capital markets. Then, real estate and gold appeared in the form of Exchange-Traded Funds, making it possible to invest small amounts.

Women managed the house with a fixed allowance every month. Now, they earn and are not accountable to anyone for money. Consequently, they spend more and invest more, depending on their level of income and mindsets.

When the whole culture and milieu changes, habits are bound to change.

I have come to understand the immense impact that our money habits have on our financial well-being. The rich clients who always negotiate interest rates, the not-so-rich who splurge with unsecured loans, and those who cannot resist a Buy Now Pay Later scheme are all part of the same society. The omnipresent push from salespersons, apps, and websites weakens our resistance.

You will find umpteen books and courses on visualization, money meditation, and money mindset which implore us to look at money as a live, responsive entity that can be attracted or repelled.

Our habits shape our relationship with money and determine the kind of financial future we create for ourselves. In this chapter, we will explore how to identify our current money habits and assess their impact on our financial well-being.

1. Reflecting on Your Financial History

To begin the process of identifying your current money habits, it is important to reflect on your financial history. Take a moment to think about how you have managed your money in the past. Did you have any patterns or tendencies that you can recall? Did you consistently save a portion of your income, or did you tend to spend it all? Were you able to pay off your debts on time, or did you struggle with repayments?

By looking back at our financial history, we can start to notice recurring patterns and habits that have been playing out over time. This reflection allows us to gain valuable insights into our current money habits and understand the impact they have had on our financial well-being.

2. Tracking Your Current Money Habits

Tracking helps, but only to understand behavioral trends. Otherwise, it is a post-event activity. What we truly need is a proactive approach.

Tracking involves observing our day-to-day financial activities and noting how we manage our money. Keep a journal or use a money-tracking app to record your income, expenses, savings, and investments.

Tracking our money habits not only helps us become more aware of how we are currently managing our finances, but it also allows us to identify any problematic patterns or behaviors.

Are you spending more than you earn? Are you consistently saving a portion of your income? Do you have any impulsive spending habits that are draining your financial resources? By tracking our money habits, we can gain a clear picture of our current financial behaviors and assess their impact on our overall financial well-being.

3. Examining the Emotions Behind Your Money Habits

Our money habits are not just about the actions we take when it comes to managing our finances; they are also closely linked to our emotions and beliefs about money. Take a moment to reflect on the emotions that arise when you think about money. Do you feel stressed, anxious, or guilty? Or do you feel excited, empowered, and in control?

Beliefs do matter because they influence our saving and spending behavior. Frugal persons may have seen difficult times and save money for emergencies. A spendthrift is probably living out suppressed dreams or wants to project a certain image.

Understanding the emotions behind our money habits is essential because it allows us to identify any negative or limiting beliefs that may be influencing our financial behaviors. For example, if we have a deep-seated belief that money is scarce and hard to come by, we may find ourselves constantly worried about our financial stability and unable to save or invest our money wisely. By examining the emotions behind our money habits, we can uncover any unhelpful beliefs and work towards shifting them to more empowering ones.

4. Assessing the Impact of Money

Habits on Your Financial Well-being

Now that we have identified our current money habits, it is time to assess their impact on our financial well-being. Look at your financial goals and evaluate whether your current habits are helping you move closer to or further away from those goals. Are your habits aligned with your financial aspirations? Are they supporting your long-term financial stability and growth?

Be honest with yourself and consider the consequences of your current money habits. Are they causing unnecessary stress and financial strain? Are they preventing you from saving or investing for the future? Are they keeping you stuck in a cycle of debt?

By assessing the impact of our money habits on our financial well-being, we can gain a clearer understanding of how they are shaping our financial future. This awareness provides us with the opportunity to make conscious choices and adjustments to our habits, to create a more positive and abundant financial reality.

Conclusion

By reflecting, on our financial history tracking our current money habits examining the emotions behind our behaviors, and assessing their impact on our financial well-being we can gain valuable insights into our relationship with money.

Through this process, we become aware of any problematic patterns or behaviors that may be hindering our financial growth. Armed with this awareness, we can make conscious choices to transform our money habits and create a financial future that is aligned with our goals and aspirations.

KEY TAKEAWAYS

1. **Reflecting on Your Financial History**

Examine past patterns and tendencies in managing money.

Assess if you consistently saved, struggled with debt, or had specific spending habits.

2. **Tracking Your Current Money Habits**

Keep a journal or use apps to record income, expenses, savings, and investments.

Identify problematic patterns like overspending or inadequate savings.

3. **Examining the Emotions Behind Your Money Habits**

Reflect on emotions associated with money, such as stress, excitement, or guilt.

Understand how beliefs influence saving and spending behavior.

4. **Assessing the Impact of Money Habits on Your Financial Well-being**

Evaluate if habits align with financial goals and aspirations.

Consider consequences, such as stress, strain, or hindrance to saving and investing.

5. **Relationship with Money**

Gain insights into the relationship with money through reflection.

Use awareness to make conscious choices, transforming habits for a positive financial future.

CHAPTER 21

BREAKING FREE: STRATEGIES TO OVERCOME NEGATIVE MONEY HABITS

To address the emotional aspects of money habits, I drew upon my background in financial coaching. I encouraged readers to reflect on their relationship with money and identify any negative emotions or beliefs associated with it. From there, I guided them through exercises to challenge these beliefs and reframe their mindset. By acknowledging and addressing these emotional roadblocks, individuals could begin the process of breaking free from their bad money habits.

In addition to addressing the emotional side, I knew that practical tools and strategies were necessary for individuals to make lasting changes. To that end, I gathered insights from financial experts and developed a comprehensive framework for systematically replacing bad money habits with positive ones.

1. BUDGETING

Budgeting is an activity many of us have undertaken in our professional lives. Fresh business targets, cost of resources, and increased level of effort are taken into account. Routine exercises involve a 15%-20% markup on last year's figures and extrapolating the graph. Companies need to do it because their balance sheets need to look a certain way and register MoM, QoQ, or YoY growth.

However, this is not the ideal way of doing it for your budget. Expenses need not always increase with income. All of us have set a minimum benchmark for our needs. While this may need to be brought down in difficult circumstances, most of the time, we adhere to it. Hence, the budget should be aligned with personal goals and values. By mapping out income, expenses, and savings targets, individuals could gain a better understanding of where their money was going and make more conscious choices. This budgeting process also involved identifying areas of overspending or unnecessary expenses and finding ways to redirect that money towards more fulfilling goals, such as saving for a dream vacation or investing in personal growth.

The envelope method is the oldest used in days of cash expenses. A household had several labeled envelopes with cash meant for a certain purpose. The heads of expenditure could be groceries, wages, school fees, utility bills, local transport, and so on.

One cannot ignore annual expenses such as insurance premiums, taxes, membership fees, donations paid to educational institutions, picnic or college tour expenses, and the cost of digital assets. It means a certain amount has to be put away every week or month in an annual expenses fund.

2. EMERGENCY FUND

An emergency fund is usually defined as an amount equivalent to 3-6 months of sustenance money. It could also mean an estimated amount for medical expenses if there are elderly or sick people in the family.

Annual expenses are well-defined, and an emergency fund is hazy. Do not mix up these two funds.

3. LEARNING AND SELF-DEVELOPMENT

Nobody can survive in this fast-moving economy without acquiring new skills. You need to have a budget for learning. Certain skills help you save money because you don't have to outsource those jobs.

Ongoing education and improvement in personal finance knowledge are as important as learning job-related skills. This involves reading books, attending workshops, and seeking guidance from financial professionals. In this digital age, I also encouraged readers to explore relevant apps and online resources that made it easy to track expenses, budget effectively, and gain insights into their financial habits.

4. ACCOUNTABILITY PARTNERS

We cannot underestimate the significance of accountability and support systems. Breaking bad money habits is not something that can be done overnight or in isolation. It requires commitment and the occasional push from trusted friends, family, or mentors. I encourage readers to find an accountability partner or join support groups where they can share experiences, exchange tips, and celebrate each other's victories.

We have been on an intense journey that required self-reflection, practical tools, and ongoing commitment. But the rewards are immense. By truly unlocking the wealth mindset and cultivating positive money habits, you can create financial freedom and ultimately live a life aligned with your truest aspirations. It was a journey worth embarking on, and I am excited to continue guiding readers on this transformative path.

KEY TAKEAWAYS

1. **Budgeting Aligned with Personal Goals:** Align your budget with personal goals and values rather than mindlessly increasing expenses with income. Map out income, expenses, and savings targets to make conscious choices.
2. **Envelope Method for Controlled Spending:** Implement the envelope method, where labeled envelopes represent specific expenses. This helps control spending on groceries, wages, school fees, utility bills, etc., avoiding overspending.
3. **Clarity on Emergency Fund:** Clearly define your emergency fund, equivalent to 3-6 months of sustenance money. Avoid confusion by separating it from funds allocated for annual expenses.
4. **Invest in Learning:** Allocate a budget for ongoing learning

and self-development. Acquiring new skills not only enhances personal growth but can also lead to cost savings by reducing the need for outsourcing certain tasks.

5. **Accountability Partnerships:** Recognize the importance of accountability and support systems. Breaking bad money habits requires commitment and occasional encouragement. Seek accountability partners or join support groups to share experiences, exchange tips, and celebrate victories on the journey to financial well-being.

Remember, the journey involves self-reflection, practical tools, and ongoing commitment, but the ultimate rewards include financial freedom and life aligned with your true aspirations.

CHAPTER 22

GOAL-DRIVEN INVESTING: ALIGNING MONEY WITH FINANCIAL OBJECTIVES

Investing is the act of putting money into assets with the

expectation of obtaining a profit or achieving a specific goal over some time. It is a powerful tool that can help you build wealth and achieve financial freedom. However, it is important to note that investing comes with risks. The value of your investments can go up or down, and there are no guarantees of returns. That being said, with the right knowledge, strategy, and mindset, you can greatly increase your chances of success.

1. GOAL-SETTING

When starting your investment journey, it is crucial to set clear goals. Your goals will serve as a roadmap for your investment strategy and will help you make informed decisions along the way. Your goals can be short-term, medium-term, or long-term, ranging from saving for a down payment on a house to funding your child's education to retiring comfortably. Whatever your goals may be, it is important to align your investment strategy with them.

Once you have set your goals, it is time to develop a long-term investment strategy. A good strategy takes into account your risk tolerance, time horizon, and financial situation. It is important to evaluate your risk tolerance honestly and consider how much loss you can withstand without it affecting your emotional well-being and ability to stick to your investment plan. Your time horizon refers to the length of time you have to achieve your goals. Generally, the longer your time horizon, the more risk you can afford to take on.

2. UNLOCKING THE POWER OF ASSET CLASSES

To embark on your journey towards long-term wealth, you must first understand the different types of investments available to you. Some common types of investments include stocks, bonds, mutual funds, real estate, and certificates of deposit. The not-so-popular kids on the block are cryptocurrency, non-fungible tokens, and structured investment products. Each investment type comes with its own set of risks and potential returns.

3. DIVERSIFICATION

It is important to diversify your investment portfolio to mitigate risks and maximize potential gains. Diversification involves spreading your investments across different asset classes and sectors to reduce exposure to any one specific risk.

When building your investment strategy, it is vital to diversify your portfolio. Diversification is the key to mitigating risks and maximizing returns. By spreading your investments across different asset classes, sectors, and geographies, you can reduce the impact of any one investment performing poorly. A diversified portfolio should include a mix of stocks, bonds, and other asset classes that suit your risk tolerance and goals.

In addition to diversification, it is important to regularly review and rebalance your portfolio. Market conditions change over time, and certain investments may outperform or underperform others. By periodically reviewing and adjusting your portfolio, you can ensure that it remains aligned with your goals and risk tolerance.

Another important aspect of investing for long-term wealth is understanding the power of compounding. Compounding is the process of earning returns on your original investment as well as the returns generated by reinvesting those returns. The earlier you start investing, the more time you have for your investments to compound and grow. By reinvesting your returns instead of withdrawing them, you can harness the power of compounding and accelerate your path to wealth.

4. RESEARCH

To make informed investment decisions, it is also important to conduct thorough research and stay informed about the market. This can involve reading financial news, analyzing company financial statements, studying economic trends, and seeking advice from professionals. However, it is important to note that no one can predict the future of the market with complete accuracy. Therefore, it is crucial to approach investing with a long-term perspective and not get swayed by short-term market fluctuations.

Finally, it is essential to have patience and discipline when it comes to investing for long-term wealth. Rome wasn't built in a day, and neither is wealth. Investing is a long-term game, and it takes time for your investments to grow and compound. It is important to avoid making impulsive decisions based on short-term market movements. Stick to your investment plan, stay focused on your goals, and trust in the power of compounding. In the end, your patience and discipline will be rewarded.

In conclusion, investing in long-term wealth is a powerful tool that can help you achieve financial freedom and abundance. By diversifying your portfolio, aligning your investments with your goals, regularly reviewing and rebalancing your portfolio, understanding the power of compounding, conducting thorough research, and exercising patience and discipline, you can build a strong foundation for long-term wealth. Remember, investing is a journey, and by taking the first step and developing a solid investment strategy, you are already one step closer to unlocking your financial genius and manifesting abundance.

KEY TAKEAWAYS

1. **Goal-Setting**: Establish clear short-term, medium-term, and long-term goals to guide your investment strategy

and decision-making.

2. **Asset Classes**: Understand various investment options such as stocks, bonds, real estate, and cryptocurrencies to diversify your portfolio effectively.
3. **Diversification**: Mitigate risks and maximize returns by diversifying your investments across different asset classes, sectors, and geographies.
4. **Power of Compounding**: Leverage the compounding effect by reinvesting returns, starting early, and allowing investments to grow over time.
5. **Research and Patience**: Stay informed through thorough research, but maintain a long-term perspective, exercising patience and discipline to navigate market fluctuations.

CHAPTER 23

AUTOMATION ADVANTAGE: SIMPLIFYING MONEY HABITS WITH SMART TOOLS

Automation is as easy as setting up auto-debit instructions on our savings accounts. The deducted money may go to a loan repayment, recurring deposit, systematic investment plan of a mutual fund, or some other scheme where you need to pay monthly amounts. Jewelers and chit funds propagate a lot of schemes with monthly payments. While assessing risk remains an important factor, it is a method of putting money aside as saving.

I will dwell a little longer on this aspect, as it takes away the burden of habits from your shoulders.

1. Save Time and Effort

Managing your finances can often feel like a daunting and time-consuming task. The sheer number of bills, payments, and transactions that need to be tracked and managed can easily overwhelm anyone. Automating these processes takes the burden off your shoulders and saves you countless hours of manual work. Once you have set up automated systems, your bills will be paid on time, your savings will be effortlessly transferred, and your investments will be consistently funded – leaving you with more time and energy to focus on your financial goals and aspirations.

2. Reduce Human Error

We are all human, and we are prone to making mistakes. But when it comes to our finances, even small errors can have significant consequences. Automating your financial transactions significantly reduces the chances of human error. By entrusting these tasks to technology, you can rest assured that your bills will be accurately paid, your savings will be faithfully transferred,

and your investments will be consistently contributed to. This minimizes the risks associated with manual handling and ensures that your financial processes run smoothly and seamlessly.
Now that we have established the benefits of automating your finances, let's dive into the practical steps you can take to set up automated systems that work for you:

3. Choose Reliable Financial Institutions

Automation relies on the trustworthiness and reliability of the financial institutions you work with. When selecting banks, credit unions, or online platforms to automate your finances, do thorough research and choose those with a solid reputation and a track record of reliable services. Look for institutions that offer user-friendly online platforms and intuitive mobile apps, as these will be key tools in managing your automated financial systems.

4. Set Up Automatic Bill Payments

One of the first steps in automating your finances is to set up automatic bill payments. This ensures that your bills are paid on time, eliminating the risk of late fees and missed payments. Most financial institutions offer bill payment services that allow you to schedule automatic payments for recurring bills, such as rent, utilities, and credit card payments. Take the time to gather all your bills and set up these automated payments, ensuring that you have enough funds in your account to cover them.

5. Automate Savings Transfers

Saving money is a vital step towards creating financial abundance. Automating your savings transfers makes this process effortless and consistent. Start by setting up automatic transfers from your checking account to a designated savings account regularly. Determine a frequency that aligns with your financial goals – whether it's weekly, biweekly, or monthly – and set the transfers to occur on the same day each time. This consistent habit will cultivate your savings mindset and bring you closer to your financial aspirations.

6. Establish Automatic Investment Contributions

Investing is an essential element of building wealth and securing your financial future. Automating your investment contributions ensures that you consistently grow your portfolio and take advantage of market opportunities. Research financial institutions that offer automatic investment plans, such as retirement accounts or mutual fund contributions. By setting up automatic transfers from your checking or savings account to your investment accounts, you will build a disciplined investing habit and watch your wealth grow over time.

7. Regularly Review and Adjust

While automation frees up time and effort, it is crucial to regularly review and adjust your automated systems to ensure they align with your changing financial goals and circumstances. Set aside time each month to review your automated transactions, reconcile your accounts, and make any necessary adjustments. Perhaps you need to increase your savings contributions, adjust your investment allocations, or update your bill payment information. By actively monitoring and refining your automated systems, you will stay on track with your financial aspirations and ensure that your finances continue to work for you.

In conclusion, automating your finances is a powerful strategy that can unlock your wealth mindset and manifest abundance in your life. By saving time and effort, reducing human error, and setting up automatic bill payments, savings transfers, and investment contributions, you can be on your way to financial success. Remember to choose reliable financial institutions, regularly review and adjust your automated systems, and stay committed to your financial goals. With a well-designed automated financial system in place, you will have the freedom and confidence to create the abundant life you desire.

Before we delve into the specifics, let's pause for a moment and reflect on the true essence of automation. At its core, automation is about simplifying and streamlining tasks and processes. When applied to your finances, this means reducing the time and effort required to manage your money and making sure that important transactions are done accurately and timely. By automating your financial processes, you free up mental and emotional space to focus on what truly matters – creating and manifesting abundance in your life.

KEY TAKEAWAYS

1. **Save Time and Effort:** Automating financial tasks frees up time and effort, allowing a focus on financial goals.
2. **Reduce Human Error:** Automation minimizes errors in bill payments, savings transfers, and investments.
3. **Choose Reliable Institutions:** Select trustworthy financial institutions for successful automation.
4. **Automate Bill Payments:** Ensure timely bill settlements, avoiding late fees, through automated payments.
5. **Automate Savings and Investments:** Cultivate consistent savings and investment habits by automating transfers and contributions.

CHAPTER 24

EXPONENTIAL GROWTH: UNLOCKING SECRETS TO FINANCIAL EXPANSION

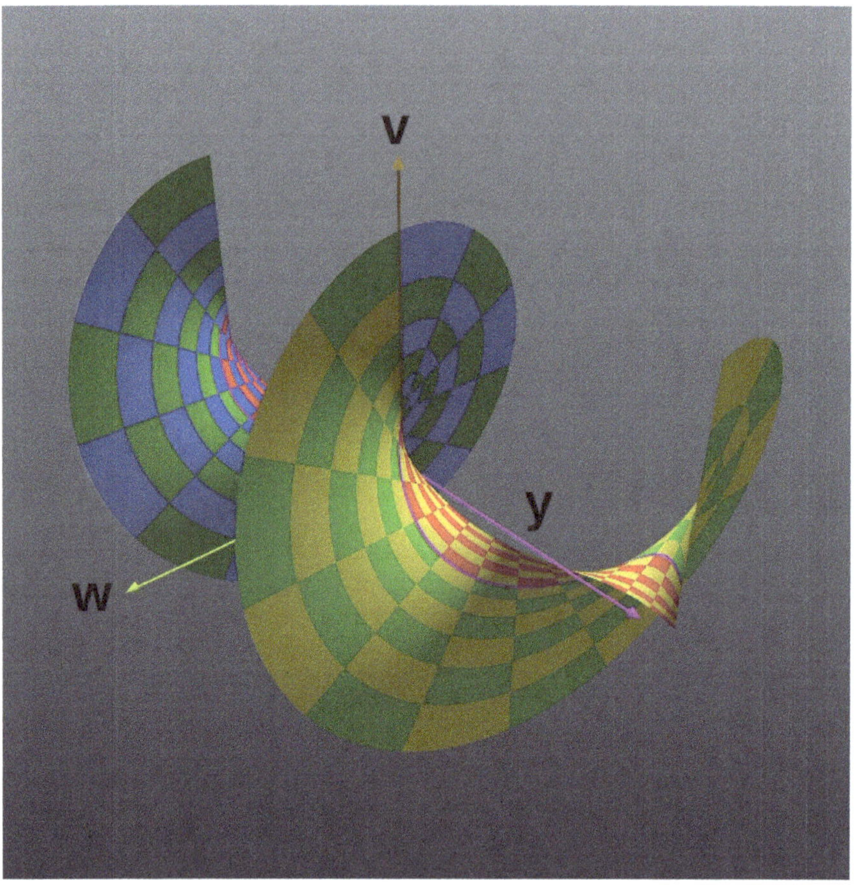

How far have you reached?

Your Money is Your Habit.

If you have less money, look at your habits.

If you have more money, look at your habits.

And yet, it's not an easy battle.

WHAT IS WORKING AGAINST YOU?

1. Addictions

Get your hands on the book "Hooked" by Nir Eyal. It glorifies the art of creating habit-forming products.

Why does everybody want to interact with you through an app? It is well known that apps have access to all the data on your device. But that's not the only thing. An app is more addictive than logging on to a website. You let the app remain on your phone, only because you are addicted to it.

So, there's a whole big industry working to make money out of you, by making you an addict.

You can argue that most of the apps are free. But the products you buy after scrolling through the apps are not free. Giving something free is only a game of getting eyeballs.

2. Small gains

We are used to thinking and planning big. The price tags on everything you want, dream, and desire compel us to dream big.

The gains through a change in money habits appear to be minuscule. So, you give it up as inconsequential. And then you go around looking for that master shot that makes you rich in a short time. Sometimes you succeed and celebrate. Sometimes, you lose more than what you invested. The loss includes everything – time, effort, and cash.

There is an alternate way of looking at it.

Compute collective gains as a family.

See what you can buy with the amount you collectively saved. Is that a bicycle a microwave or a new fancy device? Maybe you paid for your child's tuition fee with the money, and his or her academic success pays back many times later in life. Celebrate the achievements. Let everyone feel good about their contribution.

3. Power of Compounding

Our schoolteachers stopped giving us the mathematical formula for compound interest.

Relationship managers and mutual fund distributors brought it back to us with charts and graphs of how your money will grow miraculously over some time.

Remember three things about compounding benefits.

1. Start early
2. Do not break the spell by withdrawing money
3. Gains are proportional to the amount and time invested.

And one more ...

Compounding is not just about money.

WHAT WORKS FOR YOU?

1. LEVERAGING TECHNOLOGY

I fume inwardly every time I see celebrities endorsing addictive games. I wish there were policies to separate the good from the bad.

But if gamification can help you or your kids stay on course, why not leverage its power on the human mind?

Games are designed to keep a person coming back for more, by releasing dopamine and oxytocin in the system. Financial decision-making can be an interesting application for habitual gamers.

Paul Zak, a neuroscientist and a professor at Claremont Graduate University, California says

> Two core things have to happen in the brain to influence your decision-making. The first is you have to attend to that information. That's driven by the brain's production of dopamine. The second thing you've gotta get my lazy brain to care about the outcomes, and that caring is driven by emotional resonance, and that's associated with the brain's production of oxytocin. The combination of these two events is called neurologic immersion, and it is essential in helping develop new and better habits. One area where people often experience this brain state is while playing games.

2. MONEY APPS

The money apps available in the market so far are of three types

- ☐ Budgeting apps
- ☐ Expense-splitting apps
- ☐ Investment apps
- ☐ Money-lending apps

I will not recommend any app since the fintech scenario is quite fluid right now. Fresh collaborations change the nature of business, as the Reserve Bank of India keeps tightening its regulations. You can do your research as and when you want to sign on for something.

The key point here is not to give in to nudges about investing in a specific scheme or borrowing money that you do not need. Apps will drive you towards activities that are profitable for them, but after giving you some free or low-cost benefits. Make full use of the free benefits.

Some apps read your transaction alerts on SMS, and invest small change (if you have spent Rs.180/-, they take Rs.20/- to invest and round up your expenses) in digital gold or mutual funds. While this is great for creating a savings habit for beginners, the returns are not high enough to lure you into further action. But it does demonstrate how money grows, and that is a valuable lesson.

3. COMPOUNDING BENEFITS OF HABITS

I started writing for Quora six years ago and got addicted to it. There were no monetary benefits, but I gained visibility on Google, and credibility by becoming a Quora Top Writer 2018.

Quora introduced monetization. The amounts that I receive now come from views gathered on content written long back. Content does not disappear from Quora. The power of compounding is showing up.

The content writing assignments I received as a result of writing on Quora also add up.

What started as a pastime has blossomed into monetary gain.

Can dabbling with art or some other hobby get in the same category? Can it fetch money after a couple of years?

Now, pull out a calculator and compute the compounding benefits of the small amounts you save today.

Habits formed now will become a gold mine in years to come.

What you become is more important than what you save or earn, because what you become will decide whether you attract or repel money.

Rakesh Prasad

KEY TAKEAWAYS

1. **Addictions:** Beware of addictive apps designed to capitalize on your habits, as they seek to profit from your engagement.
2. **Small Gains:** Focus on the cumulative benefits of small changes in money habits, celebrating collective achievements within your family.
3. **Power of Compounding:** Understand the compounding benefits of early and consistent investments, realizing that gains extend beyond monetary aspects.
4. **Leveraging Technology:** Gamification and money apps, if used wisely, can positively influence financial habits by tapping into the brain's reward mechanisms.
5. **Compounding Benefits of Habits:** Reflect on the long-term compounding benefits of habits, drawing parallels between personal experiences (like content creation) and financial gains.

ABOUT THE AUTHOR

Reena Saxena is an author, financial coach, ghostwriter and content creator. She brings 25 years of experience in the banking and finance sector to the table.

She lives with her husband and two adorable fur babies.

She believes that a mindset lies at the core of wealth, wisdom and power. One needs to transcend beyond self-imposed boundaries to understand operating structures in the physical, mental and emotional worlds. Life happens in stories and looks so complex because of different interpretations.

Her preferred subjects in writing non-fiction are business & finance, women's empowerment, diversity and inclusion. Writing fiction and poetry are hobbies, but lend depth to articles and books.

Check out more of her writing at

https://moneygoalz.com/

https://www.reenasaxena-author.com/

https://reinventionsreena.wordpress.com/

https://sacredcircleforwomen.wordpress.com/

TESTIMONIALS

Reena is the best transformative thinker I have come across in my professional life. Here she deftly picks up our mundane acts, forces us to re-imagine and provides us a framework for bettering ourselves. Her ability to weave and storify the habits is all over the book. Go back to the first page and go ahead. This is a non-stoppable read which you will enjoy, benefit from and look forward to for her future works. Enjoy!!!

- **Lalit Bansal, a Chartered Accountant morphed into a Professional Banker.**

"Transformative Insights"

The book skilfully guides readers through self-realisation and attitude shift offering practical habits to master the wealth philosophy. The simple narrative makes complex ideas accessible while instilling a positive mindset. It is a must-read for anyone seeking a holistic approach to financial well-being.

Prachika Saxena

Human Resource Professional

Discover the transformative power of this groundbreaking book that unveils the keys to financial success by harnessing childhood habits. The author presents a compelling narrative using clear, straightforward language supported by real-life examples. Imagine a future where Master Money Habits is an integral part of the school curriculum, just like Physical Training (PT), shaping the next generation into financially empowered individuals.

Sanjay Bhargav, Former ED, Bharat Petroleum Corporation Ltd.

THE BEST TESTIMONIAL

Anil K. Saxena, a Chartered Accountant for 40+ years and a successful author says this about the book.

> Reena's book, "Unlock the Wealth Mindset" has shifted my entire being.
>
> As a Chartered Accountant for four decades, I always thought that there was nothing more I could learn about money, investment, and wealth. This book has truly shattered those beliefs.
>
> The book does not just throw platitudes. It presents a compelling thesis backed by actual science delving into the psychology of wealth as to how the deepest beliefs about money shape our reality.
>
> Having been introduced to the neural pathways of abundance, I now understand how my limiting thoughts have held me back for years.
>
> But the book is not just about getting rich. It is about living a rich life.
>
> It is not just about making money; it is about creating a masterpiece.
>
> Read this book. Change your mindset. Change your life.

ACKNOWLEDGEMENTS

Sanjay Bhargav, former Executive Director, Bharat Petroleum Corporation Ltd. for editing the book from a layperson's perspective.

Deep Saxena, Partner – Mintage Events for the cover design and delivering on very short notice.

All the beta-readers who helped me improvise the book with their valuable feedback.

Reena Saxena, a BFSI professional, financial education evangelist and coach, delves into the intricate terrain of money habits to empower you with the keys to unlock a wealth mindset. Whether you're breaking bad money habits, seeking mastery in money management, or delving into goal-based investing, this book equips you with the tools to take control of your financial destiny.

Reena Saxena

Reena is the best transformative thinker I have come across in my professional life. Here she deftly picks up our mundane acts, forces us to re-imagine and provides us a framework for bettering ourselves. Her ability to weave and storify the habits is all over the book. Go back to the first page and go ahead. This is a non-stoppable read which you will enjoy, benefit from and look forward to for her future works. Enjoy!!!

- Lalit Bansal, a Chartered Accountant morphed into a Professional Banker.

Discover the transformative power of this groundbreaking book that unveils the keys to financial success by harnessing childhood habits. The author presents a compelling narrative using clear, straightforward language supported by real-life examples. Imagine a future where Master Money Habits is an integral part of the school curriculum, just like Physical Training (PT), shaping the next generation into financially empowered individuals.

- Sanjay Bhargav, Former ED, Bharat Petroleum Corporation Ltd.

"Transformative Insights"
The book skilfully guides readers through self-realisation and attitude shift offering practical habits to master the wealth philosophy. The simple narrative makes complex ideas accessible while instilling a positive mindset. It is amust-read for anyone seeking a holistic approach to financial well-being.

- Prachika Saxena
Human Resource Professional

Reena's book, "Unlock the Wealth Mindset" has shifted my entire being. A Chartered Accountant for four decades, I always thought that there was nothing more I could learn about money, investment, and wealth. This book has truly shattered those beliefs. Having been introduced to the neural pathways of abundance, I now understand how my limiting thoughts have held me back for years.

- Anil K. Saxena,
"Passionate Chartered Accountant,
Author of a Book on Bank Audit
by Taxmann, Speaker,
Out of the Box thinker & a Plant-based food, health and fitness enthusiast."

www.ingramcontent.com/pod-product-compliance
Lightning Source LLC
Chambersburg PA
CBHW062109160726
48282CB00026B/722
* 9 7 8 9 3 3 4 0 0 6 8 6 5 *